Digital Computer Skills - Contents Page

Thank you for reading and using this book, I hope it will help you on your new journey using computer skills. All the information is my own and it is not exhaustive. There are many other sites for information which you will be able to search for when you have worked your way through this book.

There's no one way to do something, it's about finding your own way to do it.

Everything you take on after reading this book is your own responsibility. I do not take on any responsibility or risk for downloading or using any programs you have installed on your own personal computer.

I have many links to resources on my website;

www.coltechuk.com/essential-digital-skills-learning-page

CONTENTS   Page No.

INTRODUCTION TO DIGITAL COMPUTER SKILLS BOOK	3
COMPUTER HARDWARE	4
BASIC INPUT DEVICES	7
COMPUTER KEYBOARDS	7
FUNCTIONS OF THE MOUSE	14
REVIEW ONE – BASIC FUNCTIONS:	15
WHAT IS A COMPUTER?	18
WHAT IS THE INTERNET?	19
INFORMATION ABOUT EACH BROWSER	21
WHAT TO DO NEXT/ WHAT CAN YOU DO ON THE INTERNET?	22
SEARCH ENGINES	22
WHAT CAN THE INTERNET BE USED FOR?	23
WHAT IS A PASSWORD?	28
HOW YOU COULD SET UP A PASSWORD FORMULA	29
WHAT ARE COOKIES?	33
WHAT IS INTERNET SAFETY?	36
ANTI-VIRUS SOFTWARE – WHAT IS IT AND WHY DO I NEED IT?	38
REVIEW TWO – THE INTERNET:	40

REVIEW THREE – PASSWORD:	42
WHAT IS SOFTWARE?	44
WHAT IS WORD?	45
WORD EXERCISE 1:	49
REVIEW FOUR – WORD AND SOFTWARE:	51
WHAT IS SAVING?	53
REVIEW FIVE – SAVING:	57
HOW TO PRINT AND WHAT IT MEANS	59
HOW TO SET UP AN EMAIL FOR YOURSELF	62
HOW TO SEND AN EMAIL	66
REVIEW SIX – EMAILING:	68
EMAIL EXERCISE 1:	70
EMAIL EXERCISE 2:	72
WORD EXERCISE 1:	73
WORD EXERCISE 2:	75
INTERNET SEARCHING EXERCISE 1:	77
INTERNET SEARCHING EXERCISE 2:	78
KEYBOARD – EXERCISE 1:	79
INTERNET SAFETY EXERCISE 1:	80
MOUSERCISE	81
TYPING	81
HOW TO SIGN INTO OFFICE 365	82
ANSWERS TO THE REVIEWS	83
HANDY KEYBOARD PULL OUT	86
INTRODUCTION TO SHORTCUT KEYS	89
GLOSSARY	90
THANK YOU'S	96

Please use them to get you started in this most important life opening journey.

I wish you well, please persevere nothing is easy everything takes time to learn, remember you are not alone, and you will master this.

Thanks

Sarah

Introduction to Digital Computer Skills book

This book is designed to be used by anyone who would like to get started getting to know computers, how they can help carry out simple tasks in your daily life. Learn all the terms used and parts of a computer so you will become a computer user yourself.

You do not need a computer to use this book, but you may want to practice what you have learnt. You can use a computer in the library or ask a friend. Most libraries give you access to a computer so you can practice the things you will have learnt in this book.

Tips of using the book:

When something is in **BOLD and CAPITALS** you will find the full description in the **Glossary** section at the back of this book this will help you further understand the explanation and perhaps give examples to make the understanding easier.

Reviews:

I have put in reviews after each section to test to make sure you've learnt what we have gone through before moving onto the next section.

Exercises:

There are several exercises to test your knowledge, you will need a computer for most of these exercises, but please go to the local library where there are lots of friendly staff who will be able to help you.

Videos:

I have produced some videos to help with the explanation of how things work, please go to my website and watch these if you can.

www.coltechuk.com/essential-digital-skills=learning

Good luck on the start of your journey into getting to know about computers.

Computer Hardware

We will start by introducing you to the parts of the Computer. What the different parts are called, what they are referred to, and what function they carry out.

HARDWARE

There are many parts that make up a **PC** and these are called **HARDWARE**, the physical parts of a computer.

Personal Computer

When someone says PC they would usually mean the whole system, the monitor, tower, keyboard and mouse. PC actually stands for Personal Computer, and could look something like this, see left. (This actually shows a keyboard, mouse, monitor and PC).

Monitor

This is the screen, this is not the computer, think of it as a TV. There will be an on button on the front of the monitor to turn this off. It is only turning off the monitor and not the computer. They come in many different sizes. They are measured by the diagonal size across the screen and in inches, i.e. 15" screen.

Keyboard

This is an **INPUT DEVICE** you use to type commands into the PC. The keyboard is based on the QWERTY layout which was devised and created in the early 1870s by <u>Christopher Sholes</u>, a <u>newspaper</u> editor who lived in <u>Wisconsin</u> USA. QWERTY is the start of the keyboard keys is the layout of the keys on many types of keyboard.

Laptop

A laptop computer is smaller than a standard desktop computer, generally less than three inches thick. They are designed to be more portable, weigh less than desktop computers and they have mostly the same capabilities as the larger desktop computers. They can be folded flat for transporation and have a built in keyboard and touchpad, this is used instead of a mouse.

The name comes from being able to rest the computer on your lap. They come in lots of sizes of screen which can range from very small 11" up to 18" plus. They are measured by the diagonal size across the screen and in inches.

Mouse

A Mouse is an input device used to point to things on the computer screen. Select programs by clicking etc. It can come with a "tail" this connects to the computer. There are other types of wireless mice, but we will go into more details about this later in this book.

Printer

This is a device that prints out your work from a Word document or another application or the Internet. It takes the input sent to it from a PC, processes it and then prints out, it does this at high speed and is accurate.

WebCam

This is a video camera (World wide web camera – Webcam) that is connected to a computer and allows its images to be seen online. It has become very popular throughout Covid and working from home and enables people to connect to each other via video to hold meetings and catch ups. Some laptops will have them built into them.

ipad/ Tablets

iPad is a brand of tablet developed by the firm Apple. A tablet computer, usually shortened to tablet is made by many manufacturers.

Both of these are mobile devices, they are thin, they have similar capabilities to computers and smartphones but with larger screens and may not support access to a network to make calls.

Basic Input devices

Mouse

Firstly we will talk in more detail about the mouse. There are many different types of mice, ones that fit into your hand, ones that are wireless, different coloured ones, but whatever type you have they all do the same job. When you move the mouse around the desk it will move a **POINTER** on the screen of the computer. It is important to get to grips with how to use the mouse to be able to use the computer efficiently.

Computer Keyboards

Keyboards are an important input device (hardware) for the computer.

Some of you are familiar with using your phone, if you use a smart phone the keyboard opens up when you want to type something. If you look at this now you will see a similar set up to the phone keyboard, right.

Apple smartphone

Samsung smartphone

Some history of the keyboard and why it is set up as it is. The modern computer keyboard comes directly from the setup of the typewriter set up. Christopher Latham Sholes was an American who invented the first typewriter. There were various other typewriters that were invented by a number of people as early as 1714. But Christopher, along with Samuel W Soule, Carlos Glidden and John Pratt improved the simplicity and efficiency of the previous models this then led to the patent and commercial success of their invention in 1877, the keyboard we still use today.

Lots of countries throughout the world who use the Latin alphabet use the same **QWERTY** keyboard layout. Some will change the odd letter, one that is used more in their language with one that isn't used that much with a more dominant finger on the layout.

I hope you found that interesting, that's the history part done!

Here is a photo of a standard keyboard, some of the keys will move slightly around the similar area of the keyboard. If you are near a keyboard, it would be a good idea to look at it at the same time as the explanation and see if you can find the keys as we run through them here.

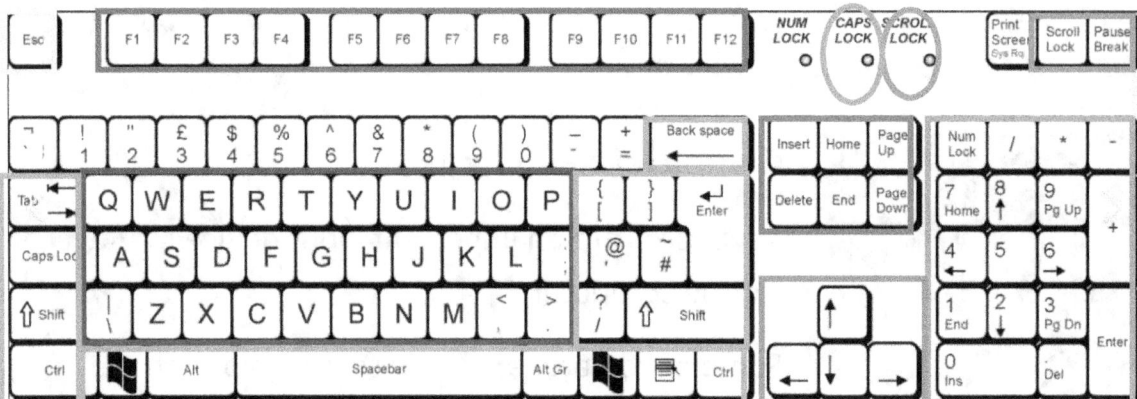

Use the keyboard pull out at the end of this book if you haven't got a keyboard to look at whilst locating the keys on the keyboard.

Here are some of the keys you will not need to know yet.

Function keys

You will not use any of these keys except the **F5** key which is used when using the Internet to refresh a webpage if it does not load properly.

Scroll and Pause Break

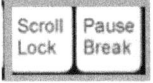 These keys are hardly ever used, even at higher levels.

These keys you will use whilst learning to use the computer.

Home keys

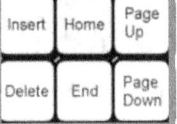 This set of keys are split into **Insert and Delete** keys; these are used to insert text into a sentence when using word to type letters. The delete key is used to delete text in sentences and to lock the screen which I will go into more details later on.

8

The **Home, and End** keys can be used in Word, Home takes you to the beginning of the document and End takes you to the end of the document. Home and End can also be used when using the Internet Home takes you to the beginning of the webpage and End takes you to the bottom of a webpage.

Esc – Escape key

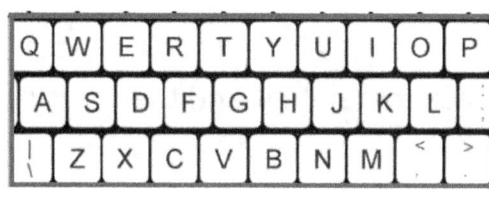 This is a useful key if you get stuck in a formula whilst using Excel (this is a program where you can use spreadsheet to work out mathematical problems), or whilst browsing a webpage to escape from a task.

Main keys

These 'keys' are the standard alphabet keys used for typing letters, words etc. When you use them, although they are shown in capital letter format, they type in lower case.

Function keys (you will need to know)

These keys work with other keys and are used to carry out a lot of different functions.

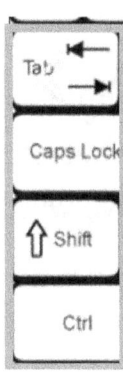

- **Tab key** – this is used to move the mouse along the page leaving gaps whilst you are using Word application. (Typing letters etc.)
- **Caps Lock key** – this indicates that any letters you type on the keyboard will be in CAPTIAL LETTERS.
- **Shift key** – this is used to type the letters on the keyboard in capitals. You hold down the shift key and another at the same time to get letters in capitals.
- **Ctrl key** – this is a very important key when it comes to shortcuts. You can press this with another key to perform a function.

- **The Windows key** - above when pressed with the E key brings up the Explorer where you can create folders and move files around.

- **Alt key** – this key is used with the Ctrl + Delete key to lock the screen.
- **Spacebar** - is the long key at the bottom of the keyboard for making spaces whilst typing.
- Alt Gr is another key used for functions, which you do not have to worry about at this level.
- Another Windows Key, same function as above.
- The paper type key is another one you will not be using at this level.
- Another Ctrl key, same function as above.
- If you click on Ctrl, Alt and Delete this will lock and unlock your screen, to unlock the screen you will need your username and password.

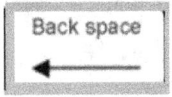

- **Back space key** – this is used a lot in typing, if you misspell a word you can back space to delete it and then carry on typing.

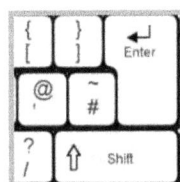

- **The Enter key** – this is used to move down to another line in Word or carrying out searches on the internet.
- **Shift key** – this is used to type the letters on the keyboard in capitals. You hold down the shift key and another at the same time to get letters in capitals.

Num lock pad

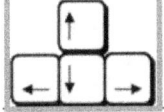

This is an area of the keyboard where you can use the number pad to input numbers. If you would like to use it you need to Press the Num Lock key and then the light (shown above with the blue circle) lights up.

Along the top line there is the forward slash which is the divide sign. The star is the times sign. Then the minus is the minus. The plus is the plus sign and then the Enter key is the equals.

Arrow keys

These are handy keys if you don't want to use the mouse to navigate around a page in Word, an Internet webpage or any other application. You can just use the keys to move up, down, left or right.

That's the keys. Now don't worry about remembering them all you will learn where they are as we go along through this workbook. But you can always come back and refer to them if you need to.

What is a digital mouse?

Let's find out about using the Mouse (a piece of hardware used when using the computer).

This is an input device, which helps us point at any item on the screen and to draw with.

This is a digital mouse

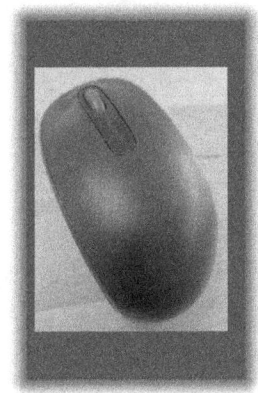

This mouse is an important piece of equipment and controls nearly everything you do on the PC.

The mouse is a pointing device with a tail. There are other mice which are wireless and would not be attached to the PC using a cable.

Mouse Pointer

As you move the mouse around on your desk the pointer follows the directions on the computer screen.

Some mice use infrared light at the bottom of the mouse, this is called an optical mouse.

The mouse works best on a mouse pad, as shown here and can be brought from many shops and comes in many sizes, some with wrist support.

Now you know about the digital mouse we can look at how to hold the mouse correctly.

How to hold the mouse correctly?

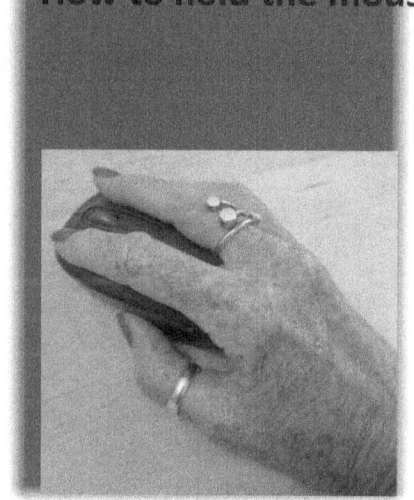

You can hold the mouse in either the left or the right hand.

You must rest your wrist on the desk.

You must not stretch too far way with your mouse.

Using a mouse mat can improve the accuracy of the mouse functions.

See my YouTube video on how to handle a mouse and the 5 functions described below.

5   FUNCTIONS OF THE MOUSE

The scrolling wheel – this usually sits between the left and right mouse button. This is known as a scroll mouse used to scroll up and down, websites and pages in Word etc.

Placing the fingers on the mouse; Index finger on the left button, middle finger to scroll and the right click.

1	Left click – this is a simple push down on the left click and release. When you do this the mouse makes a clicking noise – this is the click. The left click is usually used to select an item on the screen. It is also used in Word application to position the cursor into a sentence.
2	Double left click – this is two quick clicks one after the other with the left click. Double click is usually used to open up a file or program. You can move the pointer over to a file and then double click to open it. Do not move the mouse whilst double clicking, as this will give you another option.
3	Right click – this is a simple push down on the right click and release. When you do this is brings up a pop-up menu depending on where you are.
4	Drag and Drop – It is used to move items. Click with your left click and hold then drag the mouse to where you want it to be and release the click.
5	Scrolling – this is done with the index finger and you can roll your finger up and down the scroll wheel. You can use this scrolling when you are on any page where there is more information to see.

Once you have used the mouse for a while you will find it will become very natural to use.

Review One – Basic Functions:

Let's see what you have learnt so far about the computer.

You can choose to write the answers in the book in pencil then you can re-do this review after a month's more of practice, see how you get on!

1. Which one is a photo of a PC? Tick the correct one below:

2. How many functions are there of a mouse?

1 2 3 4 5 6 7

---

3. Can you buy a wireless mouse?

Yes   No

---

4. What combination of characters do you need for a password, circle all that apply?

Lowercase letters only

Capital letters and numbers only

Symbols, lower and capital letters only

Symbols and capital letters only

Numbers and capital letters only

Symbols, capital letters, lowercase letters and numbers only

5. Circle the items below which are hardware.

Webcam   Outlook   Excel   keyboard

Word   ipad   Internet

---

6. What are you not supposed to use when creating a password circle as many of these that apply?

Any children's ages

Your pets name   Your spouses name

Your date of birth

Your current address

Any family names   Your previous addresses

---

7. Which key do you press to make the letters capitals?

---

8. Which letter do you press on the keyboard to make spaces in between words?

What is a computer?

What can a computer do for me? Why should I learn how to use it. What can it do for me?

Make appointments
Contact potential employers
Make new friends
Find entertainment
Read news
Talk to friends
Create letters
Search for jobs
Go shopping
Pay bills
Video call with family

This is the beginning of your journey into finding out.

How to turn on the computer

You will need to click on the power button to turn the computer on. This will be on the computer and not on the monitor (remember from earlier we discussed that the monitor was like a TV and not the computer, page 7). Once you have pressed the button the computer will need time to **BOOT UP**, this lets the computer **START UP**.

Once the computer starts up you may need to **SIGN IN**.

How to sign into a computer

You may need to sign into a computer to gain access. Signing into a computer is a way of knowing who is using the PC/ Computer. It is done for security purposes in case anything occurs whilst you are using it and so the company, school, library etc knows who is using their network at any given time.

How to sign into a PC. You will need a **USERNAME** and **PASSWORD** that is unique to you.

A username is usually given to you by your firm, a public library, or another person. You are set up with a password to gain access to the PC.

What is the Internet?

This is a question you may be asking yourself right now. Or have asked in the past and was too scared to ask anyone. Here is where you are going to learn all about the Internet and what it is used for and what you can do on it.

The internet is made up of **WEBSITES**, these can be from famous names you may already know, such as Boots the Chemist (Pharmacy and Toiletries shop), Amazon (Parcels and Books), Aldi (Food shop) etc.

They have a virtual shop, a shop that is on the Internet. It sells all the same things as the shop in the high street, but you can look at the items on the computer using the Internet, order from the Internet, get the parcel delivered to your home or collection point.

Their virtual shop is called a website. Websites have pages which could be set out as below:

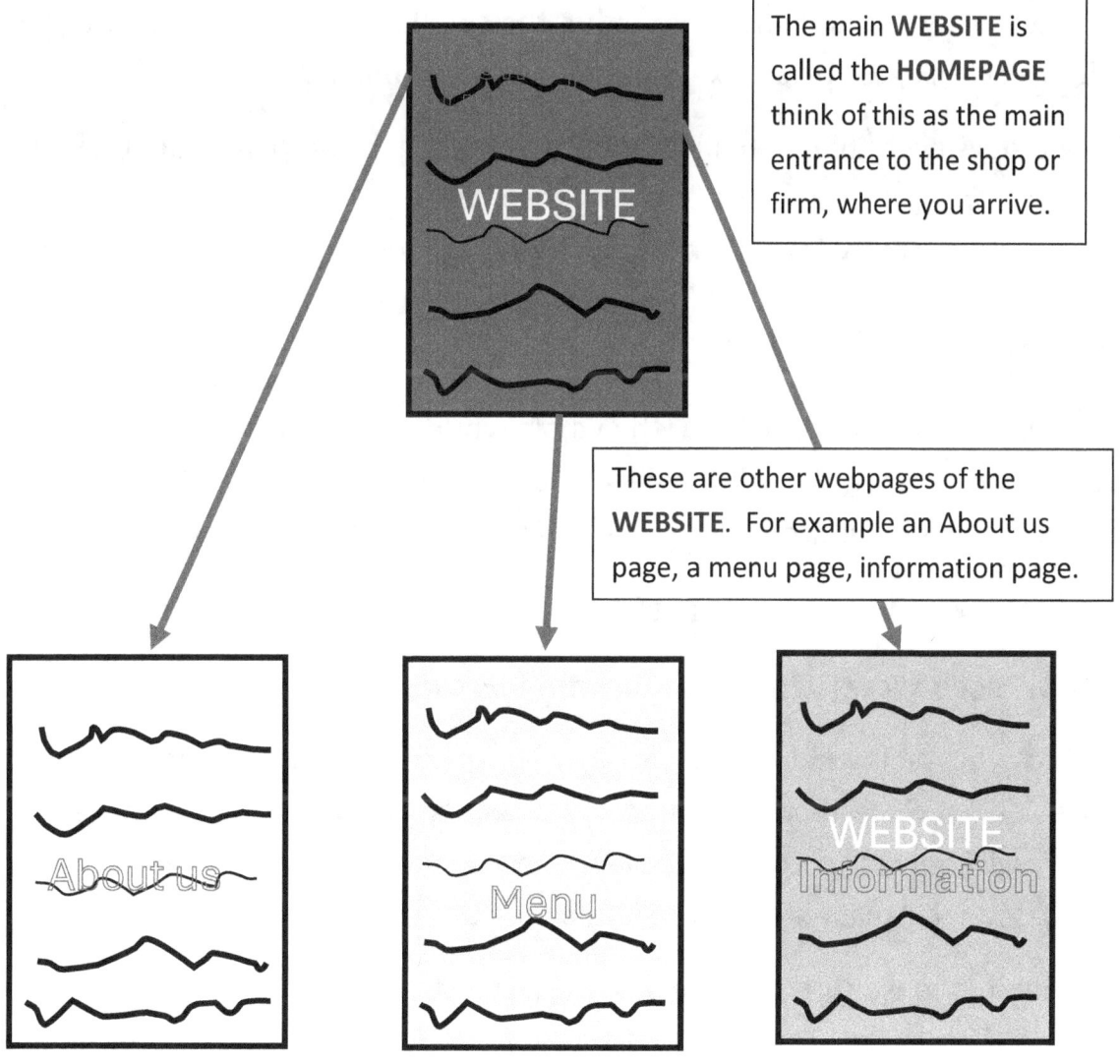

The main **WEBSITE** is called the **HOMEPAGE** think of this as the main entrance to the shop or firm, where you arrive.

These are other webpages of the **WEBSITE**. For example an About us page, a menu page, information page.

Each website can be made up of many pages, above is an example of a simple website. Each page leads off the main (Home page). There is always a way back to the home page if you get lost within the pages of the site.

Think of it as wondering around the shop, from department to department or section to section. Then you are lost, to get back to the exit/entrance you follow the exit signs.

On a website you can usually click on the company logo this is a **LINK** back to the main page (Home page). This is not always the case, as **WEB DESIGNERS**, don't have to follow any rules when designing a website.

Websites are made up of shops, companies selling services, local councils, collection societies, libraires, or any business or person, anyone can have a websites. The web address usually starts with **WWW**, then the name of the firm/company etc. and ends with either the country code *.co.uk* or *.org* or for schools or colleges, *.ac.uk* example: www.*shopname*.co.uk

Now-a-days everything is being put onto a website, if companies do not want people going into businesses or calling them, they put all the relevant information onto their website and are directing you to use this instead. So it is becoming more and more important to be able to use a computer and **'SURF THE NET'**.

The Internet is used throughout the whole world, you can look at websites from different countries, with different languages etc. You would need a company website address, or you can search for the website.

How can you use the Internet?

You will need access to a computer with **WIFI** connection.

Wifi connection is what you pay for from a provider such as BT, Virgin, Sky etc. Once you get a contract and have the connection you will be sent a router which will connect you to the Internet. You will need a wireless name/code and password usually supplied to you by the provider, which you can change3.

You need to make sure that the password is unique and not shared with anyone. This is stop other people using your Wifi who you do not want to use it, it is called to 'password protect it'. Once you have a wifi connection you can use the Internet at home.

You can always use the library computers to gain access to the Internet, a friend's PC etc.

To get onto the Internet you use what is called a **BROWSER**. There are many types you can use some of which you may have heard of, here are the most popular ones listed below.

Firefox   Microsoft Edge   Safari   Google Chrome   Opera

Information about each browser

Firefox use to be called Mozilla Firefox but is now known as just Firefox. It was voted best all-round web browser in 2023.

Microsoft Edge this use to be Microsoft Internet Explorer, voted best web browser for Windows 10 and 11 in 2023.

Safari this is known to be the best internet browser for the **APPLE COMPUTER** users.

Google Chrome is known to be the best functional browser, arguably the most common.

Opera is the most diverse browser, can be used on **PC**'s and Apple computers.

You may have a choice to which one you use to get onto the Internet, you may not. If some companies or libraries have a main one they always use, you will have to use this. It doesn't matter which one you use they all get you onto the Internet.

What to do next/ What can you do on the internet?

When you double click the browser icon you will use to get onto the Internet. It will load up and then you can start using the internet.

I have a website its **WEB ADDRESS** is the address of the company, just like in the real world every company and service has their own unique address so people can find them, using the Internet we use web addresses.

Mine is an IT Training company the address is www.ColtechUK.com

Here is the top of an example webpage:

To search the internet for a website you can use a **SEARCH ENGINE**. There are many types of search engines some of which you may have heard of.

Search Engines

These are very powerful searches that search the internet for answers. You use the search engines to search for many things you will want to find.

The Search engines you may have heard of are:

Google   YAHOO!   Yandex   Aol.

Ask.com   Baidu   Bing

Google search can also be known as Google Chrome or just Google. It is used to search and find information on the Internet using key words and phrases.

Yahoo search is also known as Yahoo. You would use this to search and find information on the Internet using key words and phrases.

What can the internet be used for?

These are some questions you may be asking and wanting to know how you can I use the Internet, below I will explain some tasks you can carry out and how it can help you in your everyday life. Here are some things you can do on the Internet when you get up and running.

- Food shopping and deliveries
- Ordering takeaway's delivered to your door
- Ordering clothes
- Booking train tickets
- Looking for places to go on holiday
- Finding out about your bin collection days
- Finding out about local schools in your area
- Looking for local restaurant's
- Applying for a driving licence
- Applying for a passport
- Your banking, transferring money and paying bills

The list is endless but as you have seen you can do lots of things on the Internet.

The Internet

What is it used for?

I will explain some tasks you can carry out and how it can help you in your everyday life.

Searching for jobs using the Internet. You will need some things to get you started.

- You will need to create a **CV**, you can carry out a search using a search engine to find sites to help you build your own CV.
- You will need to set up an **email**, see page 64.

There are internet pages called **Jobsites**. Companies with jobs advertise jobs on jobsites, you can apply for jobs on the jobsite or direct with the company.

Some popular jobsites; Reed, Jobsite, Indeed, Monster, CV-library, Totaljobs, Fish4, CWjobs.

Here is an example of how-to login to a jobsite and how to search for jobs.

We will use Indeed for this purpose although you can use any other jobsite and they all work in a similar way.

Search on the Internet for a job site, I am using Indeed, but you can use any of the examples and more above.

Or you can type in web address: https://uk.indeed.com

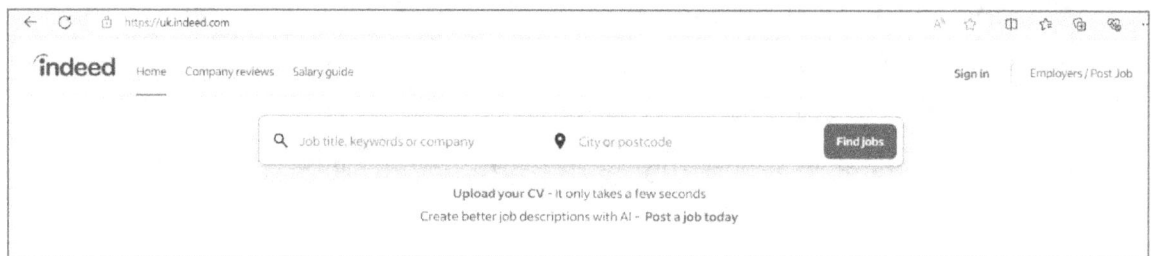

As you can see from the example here you can just type in a job title and a location and click on Find jobs and this will search its database for jobs.

Results are shown as:

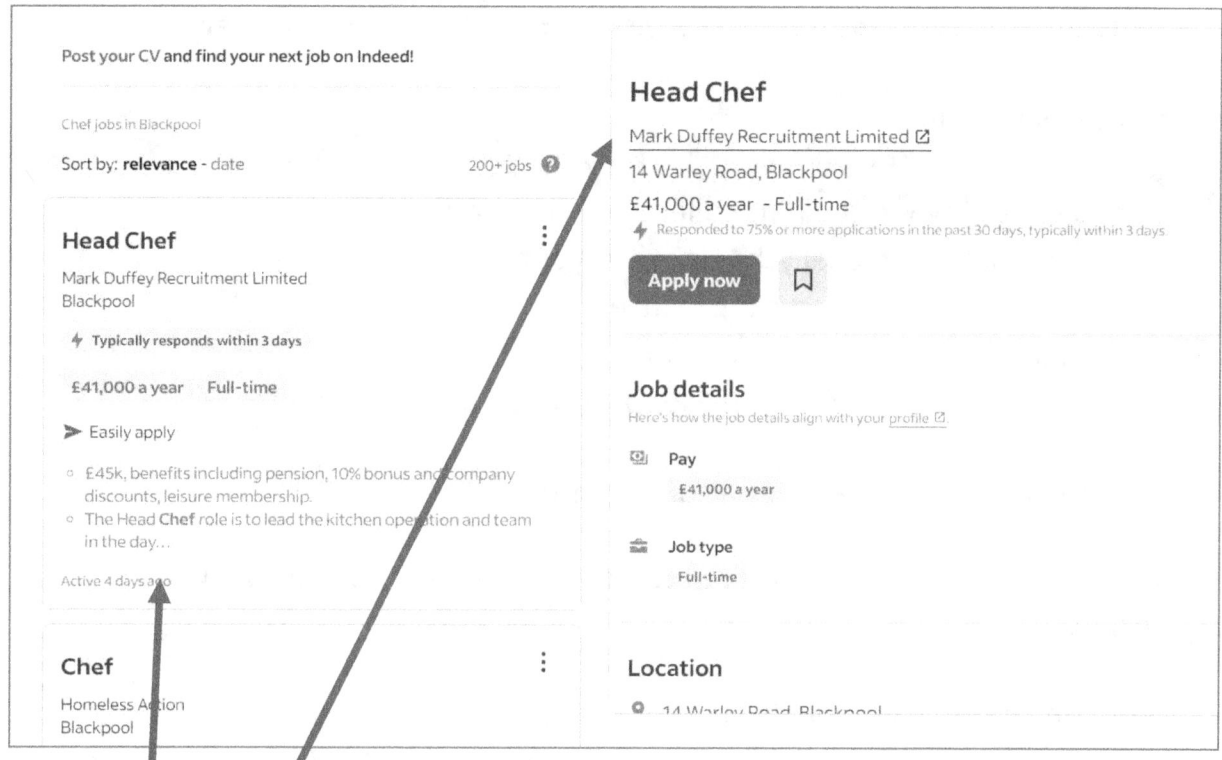

The *left-hand side* shows the job results with some basic details, who is advertising the job, how much it is paying per year, and some details about the job.

The *right-hand side* shows the job and if you wish to apply you can click on 'Apply now'.

If you scroll down more jobs appear on the page.

At the top of the page you can use the filters to narrow down the results to what you require.

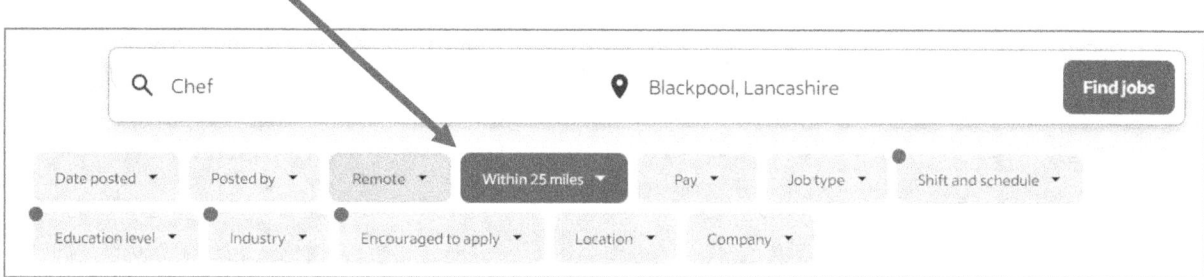

Then you have less results to look at and the jobs that show are more in line with what you require.

Searching for information on a council website using the Internet.

You can search for;

- Find out when the bins collection is next due
- Find out what local schools are in your area
- Book a visit to a recycling centre
- Check your benefit entitlements
- Find out about household support funds that are on offer

And many more services that a council offers.

Sign into your Universal Credit account and create a journal entry using the Internet.

Here are some things you can do regarding benefits;

- You can manage your benefits, payments or claim online
- You can sign into your Universal credit account
- You can sign into your Childcare account
- Manage your tax credits
- Manage your child tax credit

Shopping online, how to do it safely.

You can shop online in almost any store now a days, but you need to be careful and follow some simple rules, and always be aware of online criminals.

Everyday there are new scams, fake websites, fake email accounts and people trying to trick you into using their services and paying them money.

But there are some simple steps to follow:

- Make sure you have up-to-date **ANTI-VIRUS SOFTWARE** installed on your PC. (See page 38 on Antivirus software)
- Make sure you have a **UNIQUE PASSWORD** for every account you have online, never use the same password twice or for every account. (See page 29 on how to create a save password)
- Make sure you have use **MULTI-FACTOR AUTHENTIFICAION** when purchasing or entering your account details online
- Make sure websites have the **PADLOCK** on their site
- If something seems to good to be true, it probably is. Do not use it
- Always trust your instincts, if something doesn't feel right, Do not use it
- Is the seller a well known brand, are there any **ONLINE REVIEWS**

Use this website to get the top 5 tips the government site recommends:
5 top tips to stay safe online - GOV.UK (www.gov.uk).

I cannot be responsible for any online scams or in any way responsible for you loosing money, you need to be in charge of your own safety online.

You will need the following;

- A bank account
- An email account

Once you have read the above then we are ready to look at how to shop online.

What is a password?

A password is something that you need to use to get into certain websites. Think of it as a key to websites you will need along with a username. If you would like to shop online or use online banking or a social media account for example you will need to sign into the website with a username and password.

Before you start using passwords here is some information you will need to know.

Each password has to be unique.

The password has to contain certain elements; for example the usual set up is;

- A password must be 12 **CHARACTERS** long.
- They must contain lowercase letters, uppercase letters, numbers and symbols (symbols are &,£,?,[etc).

*They **MUST NOT** contain the following:*

- Date of birth of yourself or any members of your family.
- Names of your family.
- Names of pets.
- Favourite colours, bands etc.

Anything really that someone might know about you and could guess your password.

With this information now you can prepare to set up a password.

How to set one up?

It is always a good idea to think before hand about what you are going to use for a password. You will need them a lot, you will need lots of them once you get started online to sign into many different websites (sites).

One good idea is to set up a formula in order to remember them all. Because you are not supposed to write them down anywhere, make them rememberable or easy for a cyber criminal to 'crack your password'.

So how can you do this and still remember them. You can use a formula.

How you could set up a password formula

A password formula is something that you can set up, that is unique to yourself that is easy to remember. You may think this sounds impossible but bear with me.

What we need to include is (quick reminder):

- 12 characters
- Lowercase
- Uppercase
- Numbers
- Symbols
- Unique
- Not personal

Formulas:

This is something you can create that is unique to yourself and you can link each website you use to the same formula making the password very strong but easy for you to remember.

> # BAT08 . . .&&er

For example;

BAT is linked to a city Bath that I like, I don't go there often, nobody I know lives there and I wasn't born there.

08 is just a number I choose, I quite like 8 but nobody knows it could be a favourite of mine.

The **three dots** are going to be lowercase letters that link to the website I am going to use.

&& is just two symbols I randomly choose.

Er again is just two lowercase letter I randomly choose.

For example I am going to go shopping on Amazon online and I have to set up an account for them. They are asking for a password here is my password for Amazon:

> BAT08ama&&er

A strong password containing 12 characters, uppercase letters, lowercase letters and symbols. The ama links to the first three characters of the website I am going to use the password for, in this example Amazon.

Another example of this, I am going to sign up to Facebook so I can connect with friends online. I have been asked to set up an account where I will need a password. Here is my password for Facebook.

> BAT08fac&&er

Fac is short for Facebook. See how it is starting to work?

Another example of a formula is this:

> 06DAI(%...er

For example;

06 is a number I just choose to start my password this time.

DAI is linked to Daisy the flower that I like but not what people would know that I like.

(% is just two symbols I choose randomly.

The **three dots** are going to be uppercase letters that link to the website I am going to use.

Er is just two lowercase letters that I randomly choose.

I am going to sign up to Tesco so I can do some home shopping and get my groceries delivered to my house. Here is the password for Tesco. As you can see this is strong password that is easy to remember for me.

> 06DAI(%TESer

I am now going to sign up to Universal Credit so I can see my messages from my coach online. Here is my password for this.

> 06DAI(%UNIer

So this is my tip to you, set up a formula that is unique to you and use it for all your passwords, changing three characters somewhere in the password. Then you will have no problem remembering every password you have set up.

(At the back of this book I have put the links to website to help you with some tasks, exercises and generally helpful websites, there is one on password formulas).

When would I use one?

So once you get started using the PC, 'surfing the net', using the internet you will want to login websites. This is where you will need to set up passwords for each sign in, banking, shopping, services etc.

General usage

You should never write them down, use the same one for each site, repeat passwords etc. You shouldn't write them down in a diary in case it gets stolen;

If you use the same password for every site then a cyber criminal only needs to crack one password and then they have access to all of your sites, if your laptop gets stolen, they could get into your laptop, and then they can get into all of your banking, shopping and services sites instead of perhaps just one site.

If you think someone may have guessed your password or maybe using it, change it straight away.

What are cookies?

Have you heard about cookies, not the cookies you cook in your kitchen or buy in the shops, but the digital cookies! If you are going to use the Internet you will come across them everyday with every website you visit. They look something like this….

If you have used the Internet before now you have probably just clicked on the *'I Accept'* button and carried on using the website you wanted without giving cookies another thought. Well I am going to explain a bit about what they are and how they work.

Their formal name are **HTTP COOKIES**.

A cookie is a small piece of data from a specific website that is stored on your computer whilst you are using the website.

What do they do?

They have many functions whilst stored on your computer:

- They keep track of what you are looking at on their site, things you have looked at, how long you spent on each page etc.
- This is so they can send you targeted adverts for goods or services they think you might find useful.
- You might be looking for a Disney costume for your child in the morning and then later on that afternoon when you are back on the computer on another website and there will be adverts for Disney costumes, this is because of the cookies.
- Remembering your login details.
    - This means that you can log into a site, **FACEBOOK,** for example, and then close it down and later open up a webpage and Facebook and you will not have to log in again, the cookie remembers you.
- Keep track of how many visitors a website has for the website owner.
- Tracking your activity.

Tracking your activity;

This can be a very helpful or it could breach your privacy, this all depends on how the website you are browsing on uses your information and how the data is collected. This is why you get the notification about cookies because now they have to tell you what they are going to use your information for.

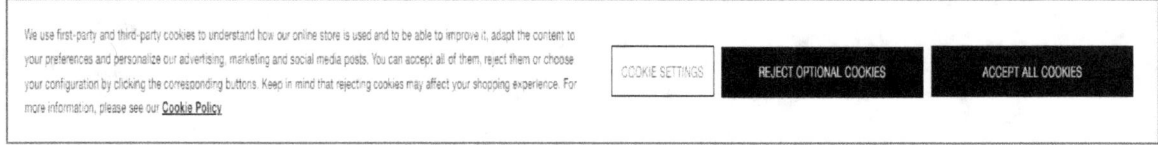

How does the cookie work?

I will attempt to explain this in simple terms so you can understand it simply.

When you visit a website the website puts a cookie onto your PC, each PC has its own **COOKIE ID CODE** the website then uses this ID to keep a track of your visit to the site.

The reason it does this is:

- To keep items in your shopping trolley
- Which items you have looked at so it can suggest similar items for you, giving you a better shopping experience
- To save vouchers or discounts that can be used later

They have more functions, but these are just a few of the common ones.

Breaking down the Cookies

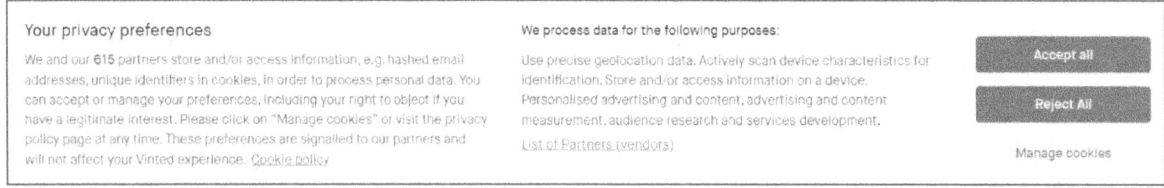

Cookie policy above.

Manage cookies – first thing you will see is the privacy policy, example below taken from a website:

About Your Privacy

We process your data to deliver content or advertisements and measure the delivery of such content or advertisements to extract insights about our website. We share this information with our partners on the basis of consent. You may exercise your right to consent, based on a specific purpose below or

If you choose to manage the cookies you will get options as to what information the website can collect.

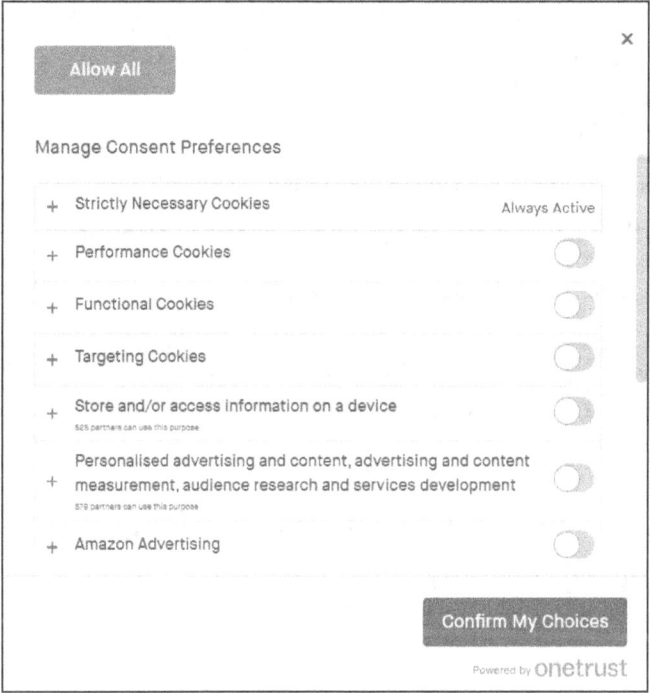

Here left, is an example of the options you could choose.

You can see they have **Strictly Necessary Cookies** which you can't opt out of. If you don't want the site to collect any data and in their cookie policy this is always active you will have to choose not to use the site.

Every cookie policy will vary but will be also very similar to the options you will be shown.

They are generally used to make sure you have a more enjoyable experience whilst you are using the website.

What is Internet Safety?

Working safely online means to stay safe whilst using the Internet, shopping, banking, surfing etc.

How do you stay save online? Here are some tips to follow.

Shopping online:

If you intend to shop online you will need to sign into the shop's website, with a username and password, as discussed previously.

To stay safe online you must **never use the same password twice**. Never share a password or make up the password using anything personal, family names, date of births etc.

When shopping online always **check there is a padlock symbol** in the web browser window when you are logged in or registered. The **website address should begin with https://**. The 's' stands for secure.

Example:

Remember to log-out of your accounts when you have finished your shopping. This is especially important when using a public computer, at college, work, library and friends house etc.

Secure your Wifi:

If you have **Wi-Fi at home you must make sure it is protected with a strong password** that only you and your family know. When you are out and about, never use an unsecured **HOTSPOT**.

Emailing:

When you **receive a message that looks suspicious never open it** or forward it to anyone else, delete it or report it as phishing.

Do not respond to a social media message from someone you don't know.

Protecting your devices:

When using a computer on the internet you will need to make sure you have **ANTI-VIRUS SOFTWARE** installed on your computer and you keep it up to date. This will protect your computer from **VIRUSES** and **HACKERS**.

Bidding on auction sites:

If you use Auction sites make sure you never transfer any money directly to a bank account but make sure you make payments through the auction site.

Social media:

Check your **PRIVACY SETTINGS** on all your social media accounts so that only the people you want to share information with can see it.

If you are a victim of online fraud, report it. This way we can all help to make the internet a safer place. www.actionfraud.police.co.uk

Important things to remember!

- If something looks too good to be true it probably is, don't like it click on it or forward it to anyone, delete it or report it.

- Make sure your anti-virus software is always kept up to date.

- Look for the padlock whilst banking, shopping or entering any personal details to make sure the website is secure.

- Always report any **phishing** or suspicious emails, websites, posts etc to: www.actionfraud.police.uk

Anti-Virus software – what is it and why do I need it?

Anti-virus is a program which is designed to protect computers, laptops, tablets or other electronic devices from potentially harmful viruses, **MALWARE** and threats.

Let's start by asking you some questions:

Do you know how a hacker can gain access to your data?

Weak passwords, weak security questions, writing down passwords, no anti-virus software, not updating your computer, not using secure websites etc.

What information do you have stored on your PC?

Things could include; photos, documents, personal information, passwords, insurance policy details etc.

What online services do you use?

Social networking, travel websites, video streaming websites, online games, news sites, emailing etc.

Once you start using the computer you will have, as above an example of the information you could have stored on your PC.

How do you or could you keep this information safe?

Use strong passwords

Don't use the same password twice

Use two step authentication

Use strong security questions

Having up-to-date Anti-virus software

Keeping your computer up to date with updates

Anti-virus software choices

There are many anti-virus software programs on the market you can purchase. It could be difficult to choose the right one for you but there are many sites that give you comparisons of the most popular ones.

I will give you some examples of where to head once you are ready to purchase the software.

Here are some sites to choose from for the best anti-virus software. Use Google, Bing or another search engine to search for these websites:

Best Antivirus Software (antivirusguide.com)
This gives you the top 5 best anti-virus software

UK - Antivirus (top5antivirus-software.com)
This gives you the top best anti-virus software

Best antivirus software 2024 for PC and Mac | TechRadar
Top 10 anti-virus software for the PC and **Mac**

Once you have installed the software on your computer it is important to make sure you know if it is updating itself or if you need to check on updates you may need to install on the software. As out of date anti-virus software will not be keeping up to date with the latest virus and thus making your computer vulnerable to viruses and hackers.

Review Two – The Internet:

Let's see what you have learnt so far about the Internet.

You can choose to write the answers in the book in pencil then you can re-do this review after a few month's more of practice.

1. Name any web browser you can use to get onto the internet and search, write it below:

---

2. What items do you need in order to keep yourself save when shopping or banking online? Circle any, you can do as many as you like.

Printer Paper

Secure password

Email address

Up-to-date Anti-virus software

Mouse

Username

Unique Password

Padlock

Software

Printer

---

3. What is a homepage? Circle the correct answer.

The Homepage is the main page of a website where all the details of the company are found.

You can use this to search for anything on the Internet.

This is where all the passwords are all kept for the company.

Somewhere you can go to on the internet to find out information about where people live.

40

4. The Internet is only available in the UK, true or false?

   TRUE   FALSE

5. Google is a web browser?

   TRUE   FALSE

6. List the web browsers you can remember below.

7. You can't use the internet on your phone.

   TRUE   FALSE

Review Three – Password:

Let's see what you have learnt so far about what a password is.

You can choose to write the answers in the book in pencil then you can re-do this review after a few month's more of practice.

1. What things do you need to include within a password? Write as many answers as you can remember:

   ----

2. What must you not include in a password to make sure it is always secure and hard to guess? List everything you can remember below:

   ----

3. When do you need to use passwords, select all the sentences below that this applies to.

   When you enter the library

   When you log into your bank account

   When you want to write a document on Word

   If you are going to send someone an email

Logging into your Outlook/Email account

When you are browsing on the Internet

---

4. Which sentence is the best sentence that refers to passwords?

    Your password must always be long with no mention of your personal details

    You should use your families names within a password so you can remember it

    You should always include your partners name and your favourite colour in your password

---

5. How can you remember your password, what is the best way to set one up? Explain in as much detail as you can.

---

6. Circle the best practices for having a secure password.

    Use a password manager   Use your children's names

    Write down the password
                                    Use a password formula

    Use the same password for all logins

    Use a password that is easy to remember but hard to crack

What is software?

Software is a set of instructions that tells a computer what to do. The hardware is the physical parts of a computer whereas the software is the instructions that send the computers hardware tasks to perform.

There are two main types of software, one is the system software which sets up the PC, tells it how to run the computer etc. and then there is the application software which is what you will be using as a new starter to using computers, application software is things like Outlook, Word, Excel etc.

If you currently use a smart mobile phone you will probably have downloaded apps for your phone and these are tools or (application software) that you use to carry out different tasks.

With a computer you will use applications (apps) to carry out different tasks too. For example see the table below for details of popular application software.

Application name	What it is used for	Where you can get it from
Word	Used for creating letters, documents, memos, essays, homework etc.	You can sign up and buy a subscription from Microsoft Office.
Outlook	Used for sending and receiving emails, booking calendar events etc.	You can sign up and buy a subscription from Microsoft Office.
Anti-Virus	Used for keeping your computer up-to-date against viruses that can harm your data and PC.	Found online, there are many companies offering these services, search for best anti virus software and work out the best one for you, see Anti-Virus.
Excel	Used for creating spreadsheets, doing VAT, accounts and calculations etc.	You can sign up and buy a subscription from Microsoft Office.
PowerPoint	Used for creating presentations, leaflets, flyers, posters, certificates, invitations etc.	You can sign up and buy a subscription from Microsoft Office.

What is Word?

Word this is a **MICROSOFT** product part of a collection of software programs you can use to carry out a variety of daily tasks.

When using Word you can write documents, format documents, create documents, CV's, write up assignments, create books, articles and much more.

How to open up Word

If you are using a public PC (in a library or a support centre) there are a few places you will be able to find Word. If you have your own PC you may not have access to it. In this case you could sign up to use Office 365, see page 83 for details on this.

One way to see if you have Word is to;

1. Click on the windows key on the keyboard or as shown here on the bottom of the screen.
2. Use the mouse to scroll through the programs that are listed there in alphabetical order so Word will be at the bottom of this list.
3. Click on this and Word will open up.

OR

1. The Word icon could also be on the task bar at the bottom of the screen.
2. If it is here click on it and it will open up.

OR

1. You could find the Word shortcut icon on the Desktop of your computer.

You will see on the page the flashing cursor as below, this shows you where the typing will start.

| | Cursor on the page. | | Pointer you can move around a page to insert text into a page. |

To type onto the page using the keyboard. The cursor should be flashing on the page, as above, when a new page is selected and all you have to do is start to use the keyboard and then you will see your typing on the page.

Practice typing this sentence onto the page:

This is my first time typing using Word, I hope to learn more and more about this package, whilst typing up my notes using Word.

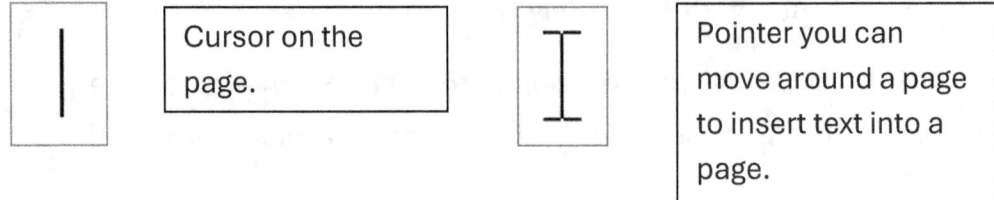

If you type up this text above with a spelling mistake you will see this red zigzag under the word, as right. This means you have a possible spelling mistake, if you right click on top of the word you will get some options as below;

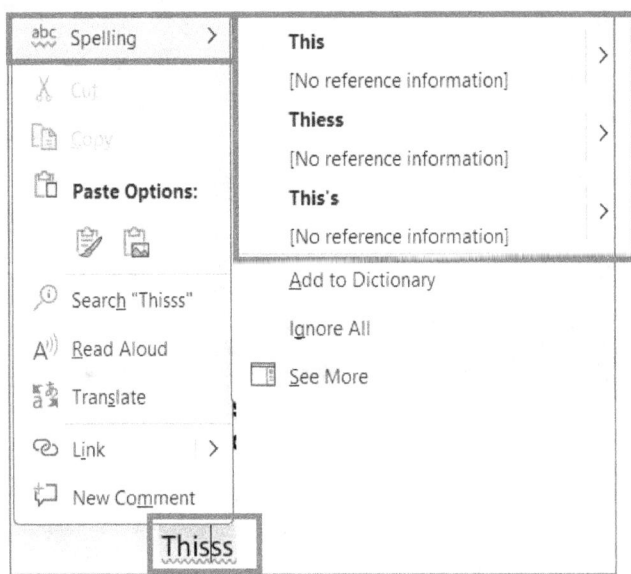

To select the correct word just left click on top of the word and it will change the mistake to the correct one you have chosen.

If you type up the text and you get a double blue line underneath, as right, then this is a possible grammar mistake, again if you right click on top of the word, you will get some options as below;

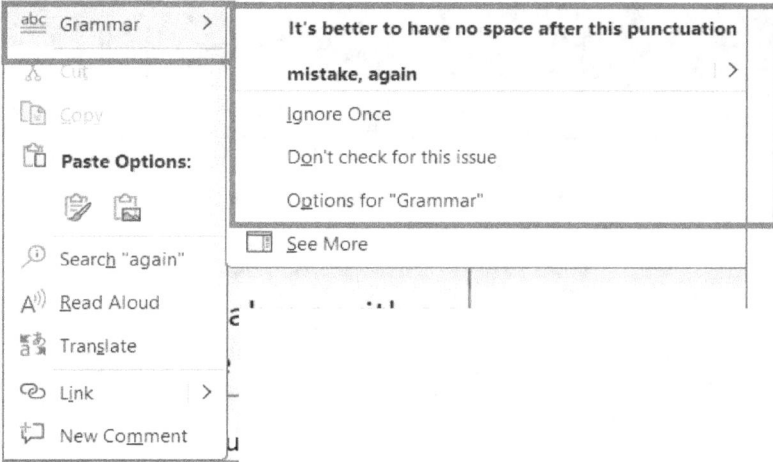

Again as the spelling, click on top of the correct word and it changes within the text.

Take out and use the handy keyboard layout plan at the back of this book to help you use the keyboard and find the correct keys for typing.

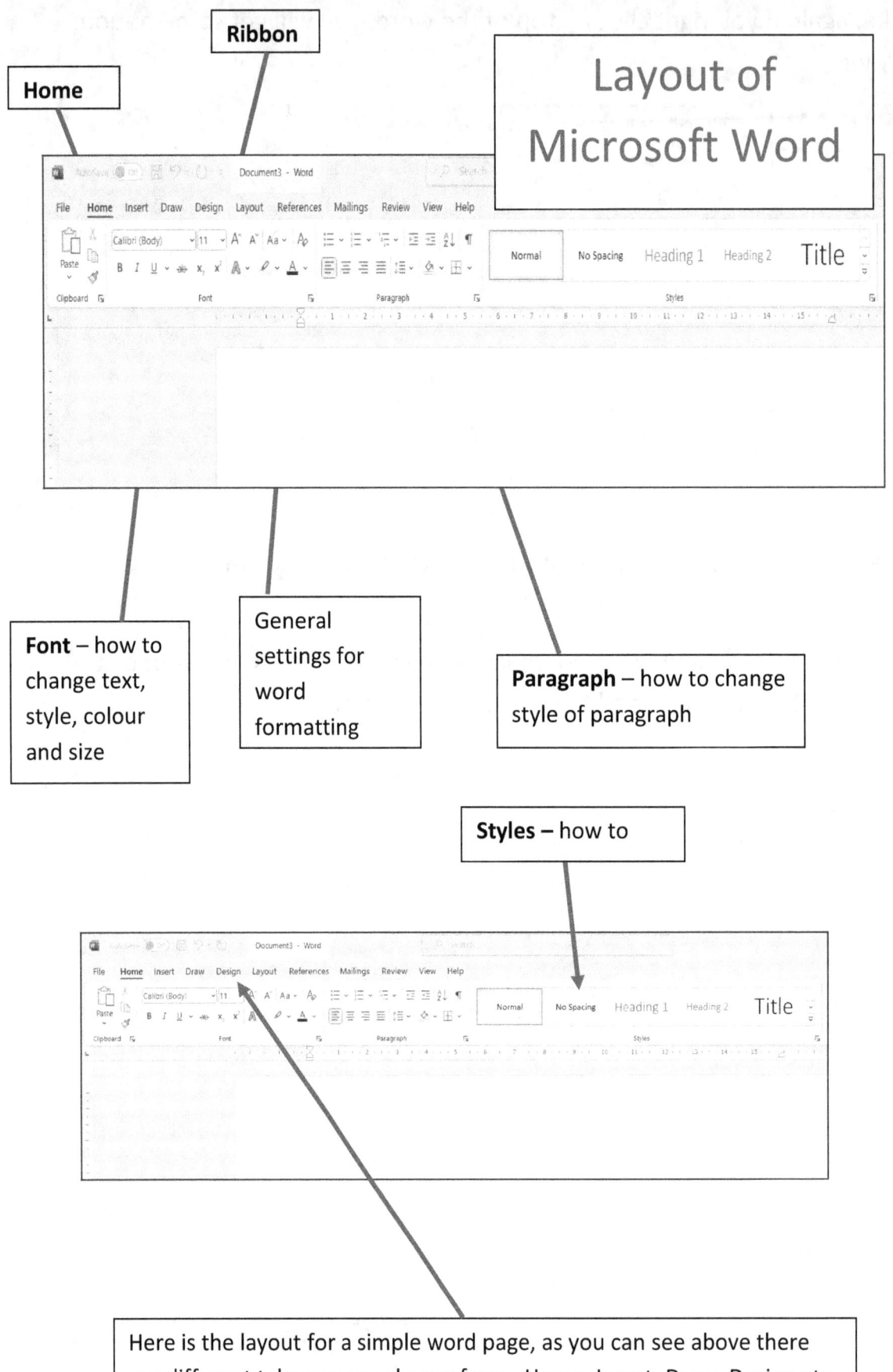

Layout of Microsoft Word

Home

Ribbon

Font – how to change text, style, colour and size

General settings for word formatting

Paragraph – how to change style of paragraph

Styles – how to

Here is the layout for a simple word page, as you can see above there are different tabs you can choose from. Home, Insert, Draw, Design etc.

Word Exercise 1:

Carry out this exercise to practice your word skills.

1. Open up a new word document, File, Blank document.

2. Type up the following into word –

What feels like fun to me, but work to others? The mark of whether you are made for a task is not whether you love it but whether you can handle the pain of the task easier than most people.

3. Check in the Home ribbon and the font section to see what font you are typing in and the font size.

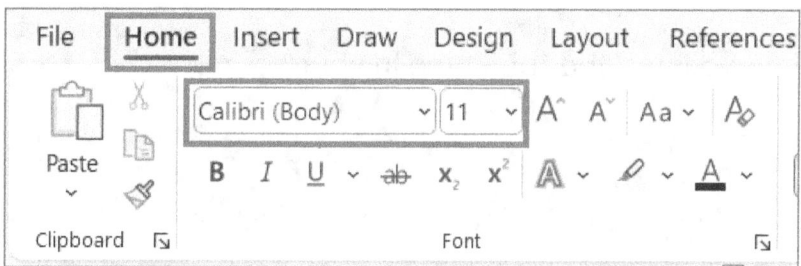

4. Type on the next line what font you are using and the point size, i.e above is Calibri (Body) point size 11.

5. Then change the font style to another font style by click on the down arrows next to the text, indicated by the circle on the ribbon below.

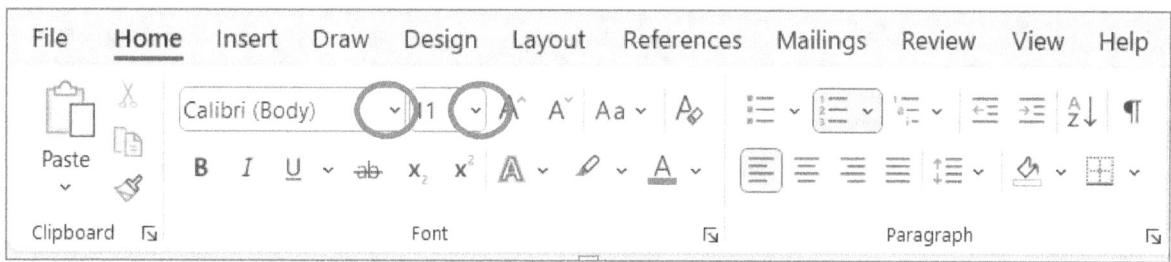

6. Type up the following text in the new font and style.

I cannot express how important it is to believe that taking one tiny—and possibly very uncomfortable—step at a time can ultimately add up to a great distance.

7. Next type up a title as below and centre it at the top of the page.
   To centre text use the Paragraph section on the Home Ribbon, highlighting the text first.

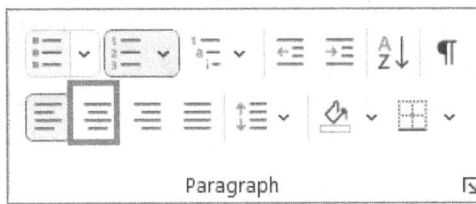

This is the first write up I have completed in word

8. Go to the bottom of your text and insert a photo, one of your choice; Insert, Picture, Online Pictures.

9. Move down the page two lines and then type in your name.

10. Print out the page, File, Print, select printer and then click on Print.

Review Four – Word and Software:

Let's see what you have learnt so far about Word and what it does.

You can choose to write the answers in the book in pencil then you can re-do this review after a few month's more of practice or just go ahead a give it a go!

1. Where can you find MS Word?

   Under the Windows key   In Excel

   Pinned to the taskbar   Shortcut on the desktop

   In the cloud   On the BBC webpage

   On the Printer

---

2. Does Word have a spellcheck?

   Yes   No

---

3. Circle the words below that are software packages?

   Word   Printer   PowerPoint

   USB stick

   Removable storage   Outlook

   Computer Desktop   Excel   Google Drive

4. What are all these?

Calibri, Times New Roman, Arial, Bookman, Sans Serif

----

5. Which one of these symbols will centre text on a page?

6. Which one of these symbols will make the text you are typing italics?

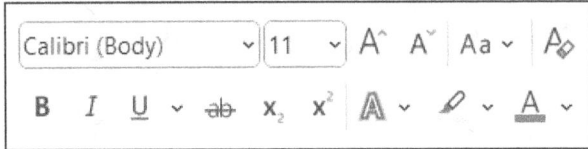

7. Which one of these symbols should you click to change the font colour?

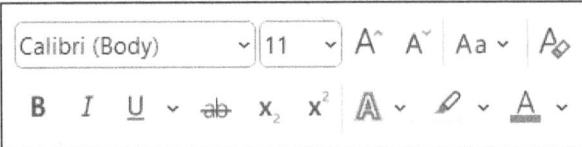

8. Which tab will you find this, where you can insert photos onto a document?

Please see the answers on page 85

What is saving?

When you use certain software programs such as Word, Excel PowerPoint to name a few you will be creating a word document, an excel spreadsheet or a PowerPoint presentation. If you start working on a document one day and would like to finish off the next you will need to save the work somewhere to use the document to again tomorrow.

Where can you save?

There are a number of different places to save to, take a look at the diagram below for the places and then I will explain below where they are and the best places to save.

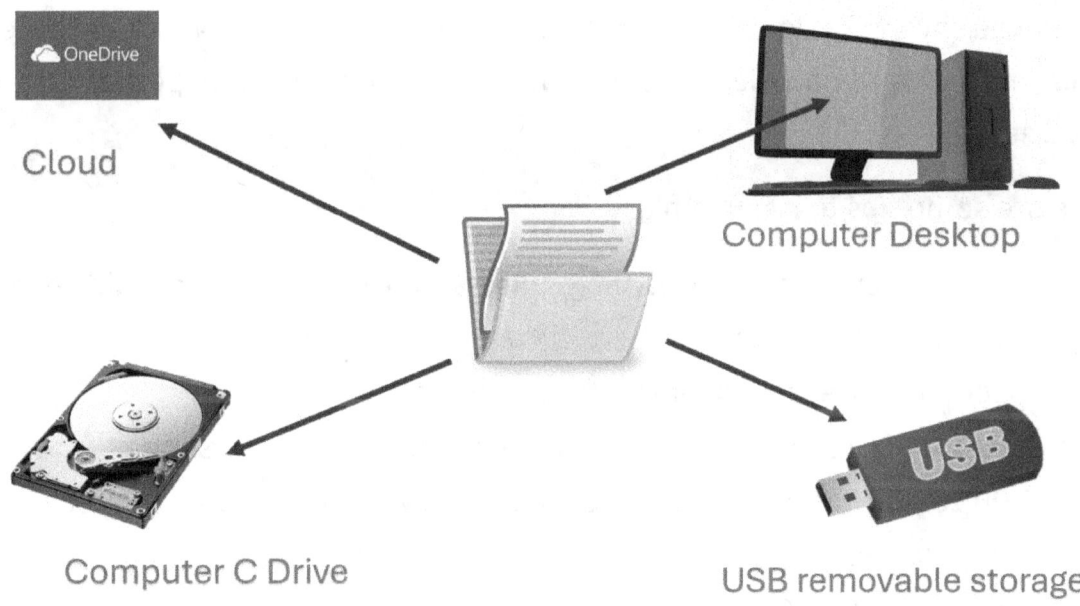

Cloud Storage – this is said to be "on the cloud" data is remotely stored in multiple servers which is accessible to users over the internet. These cloud storage providers (such as Microsoft OneDrive, Dropbox), are secured, protected and data is easily accessible and available to you. You can access this from your personal computer, your friend's computer or the library wherever you like across the world.

Computer C Drive – this is the Document store on your computer, where you can create folders and save files and staying organised etc. If you store here you need to make sure the files are **BACKED-UP**.

USB Stick – This is a portable storage place you can save files to. You can create folders and get organised, taking the files with you in your pocket and using them somewhere else. The disadvantage is you can lose the USB Stick, or the stick could get corrupted with a virus.

Computer Desktop – this is the desktop of your computer, and it is probably the worst place to save a file. This is because it is unorganised, and you can only access it when you are on that computer. It also makes it hard to find if you have many files saved to your desktop.

What can you save?

You can save anything you create within a software program. You can access it again later with one of the examples above.

Get organised:

When you save a file you will need to remember where you saved it to retrieve it again later. It is a good idea to save it with a memorable name, perhaps the date or something else.

Here are some tips to naming files:

- Be consistent with your naming, think about anything that could change over time or location
- Use lowercase letters, or capitalise names
- You should keep file names to between 25-35 characters long
- You could consider leading the file names with 0's or some sort of numerical filing order
- Use numbers or letters but do not use symbols or spaces
- If you wish to separate names you can use hyphens or underscores

Some examples of filenames you could use:

001_letter_Mr_Smith

Letter-mr-smith

Letter_Mr_Smith_24.03.24

Folders:

Folders can be created to organise your storage and make finding files easier to do. For example you can create folders for different topics, different months, work projects etc.

You should create your folders before saving. To do this open up the File Explorer, click on the yellow folder on your task bar:

Or press on Windows key and E, this also opens up your File Explorer.

Here is example of a file explorer.

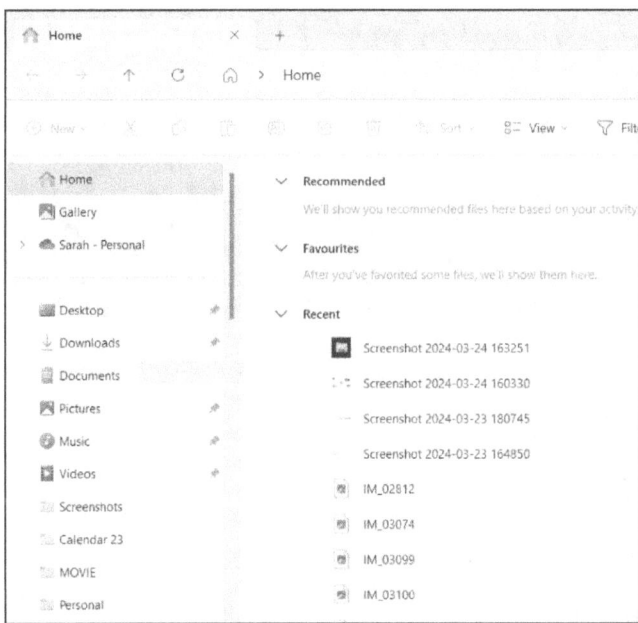

Here is an example of my file explorer above the yellow folders are the folders, to create a new folder follow the instructions as below.

To create folders go into the Desktop, or your C Drive or if you have a OneDrive go into this. You then have the option New, Folder. This will be created where you have indicated.

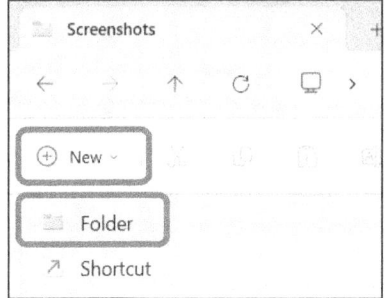

or you could always right click in the file explorer and click on new folder.

You can save in Word, Excel, PowerPoint etc. Each of these software programs follow a very similar format.

Word example:

You are in Word and carry out some work and would like to save. You have already created a folder and called it XXXXX.

Select File, Save a copy, or Save (whichever is showing in your Word package).

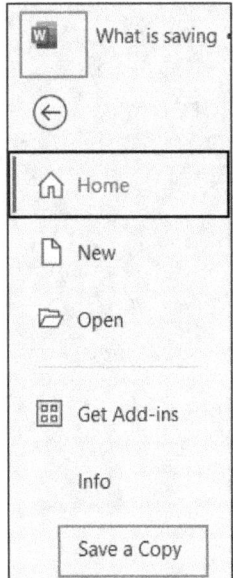

Choose an area you wish to save into;

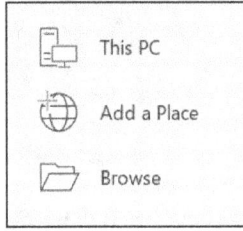

This PC – your hard drive on your computer.

Browse – from here you can browse to a cloud storage (e.g. Dropbox), USB stick etc.

You can follow this system in Excel, PowerPoint and other packages etc.

Try it out!

Review Five – Saving:

Let's see what you have learnt so far about Saving.

You can choose to write the answers in the book in pencil then you can re-do this review after a few month's more of practice or just go ahead a give it a go!

9. Circle the items below which you can save from.

Word   PowerPoint

Printer   Excel   Computer

Tracking   Outlook

Digital skills   Cloud storage   Cookies

---

10. List all the places you can save to.

---

11. Which of these are cloud storage?

C Drive   Box storage   DVD

Drop box   USB stick   Office 365

Google Drive

Computer Desktop   Removable storage

12. What can you do with removable storage? Choose the correct answers.

- You can take it away and use it in another computer

- Can be a good way to back up your files

- If you save onto the PC your files will be backed up

Please see page 82 for answers.

How to print and what it means

Printing is the process of producing the text and images you have created on the computer and printing them onto paper. Printing is done through a printer, you will need to have a printer, the printer needs to have ink, usually black and colour, and also paper.

The printer can be connected to your computer or you can have a printer connected to the internet (Wi-Fi) and you can print from any computer you have in your house or flat etc.

To use the printer you will have to install the **PRINT DRIVERS** for the printer. These are found on the internet, you need the name of your printer and then search for the drivers on the internet, install them and then you can print to the printer.

Within Word, for example, here is how you would print your document.

File, Print:

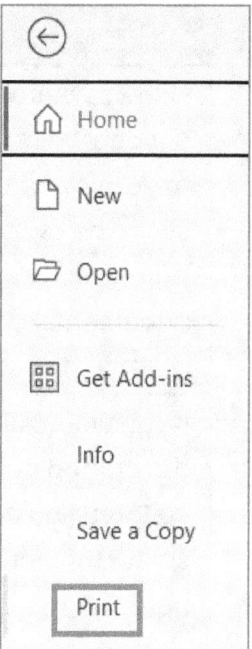

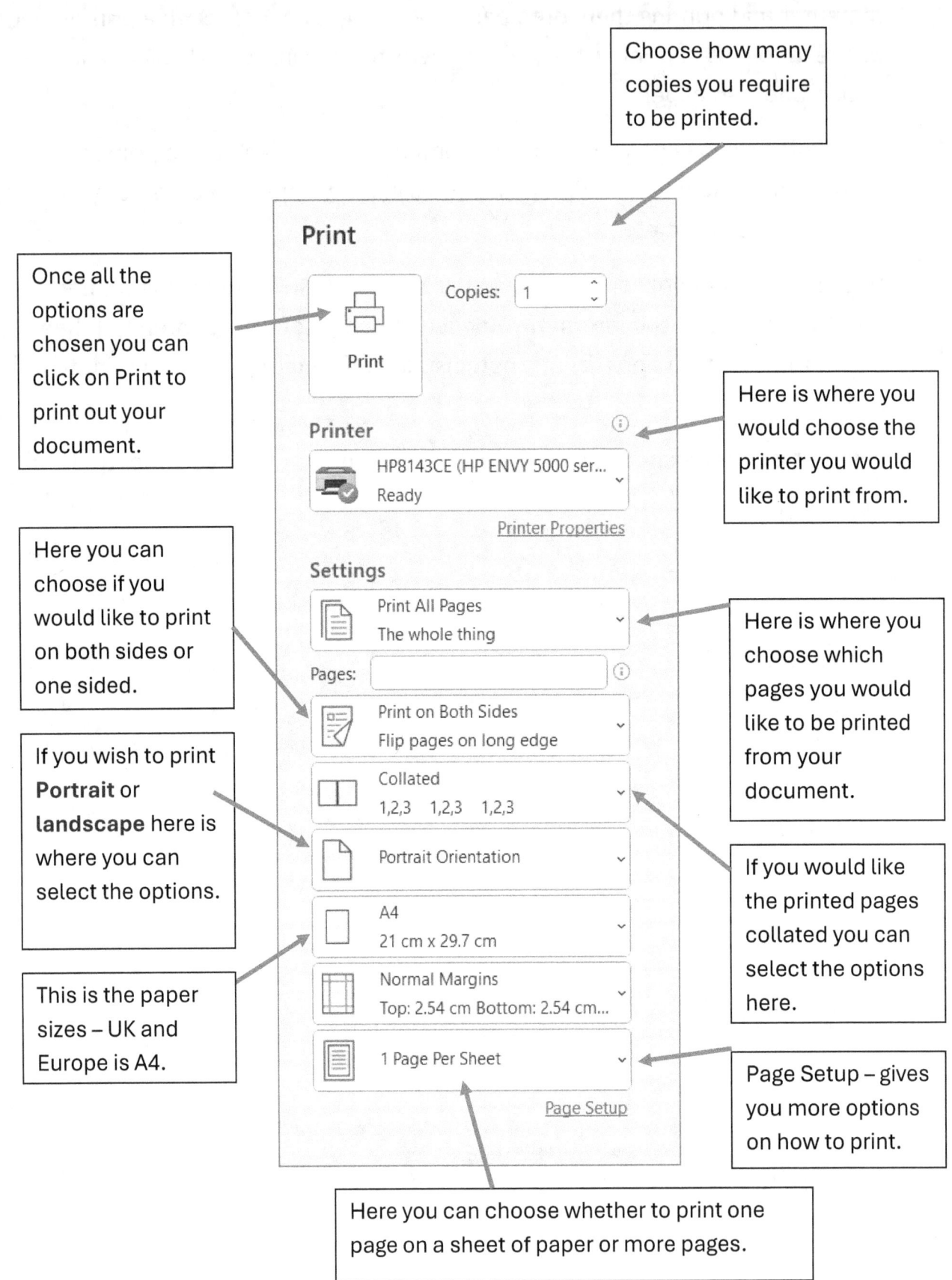

Choose how many copies you require to be printed.

Once all the options are chosen you can click on Print to print out your document.

Here is where you would choose the printer you would like to print from.

Here you can choose if you would like to print on both sides or one sided.

Here is where you choose which pages you would like to be printed from your document.

If you wish to print **Portrait** or **landscape** here is where you can select the options.

If you would like the printed pages collated you can select the options here.

This is the paper sizes – UK and Europe is A4.

Page Setup – gives you more options on how to print.

Here you can choose whether to print one page on a sheet of paper or more pages.

What is an Email?

An Email is an electronic mail, it's an instant messaging service between the person sending the message and the person receiving the message.

You can send written messages, non-text messages like images (Pictures), Videos and sound files.

For most sites you will need an email address if you wish to use the Internet.

An email is made up of a variety of items as explained below:

Example of emails:

Email provider you have chosen to use as your email.

joebloggs@gmail.co.uk

username, sometimes related to your name.

Country code for where your email is based.

Paulsmith@hotmail.com

Who is the **Email provider** for this email?..

What is the **Username** for this email?………………………………………..

What is the **Country Code** for this email?..

Geetapatel@yahoo.au

Who is the **Email provider** for this email?..

What is the **Username** for this email?………………………………………..

What is the **Country Code** for this email?..

To be able to have your own email you will have to sign up for one. There are a number of different providers out there here are some of the most popular ones and their email addresses.

Yahoo	www.yahoo.co.uk
Hotmail	www.hotmail.co.uk
Outlook	www.outlook.com
Gmail	www.gmail.co.uk

How to set up an Email for yourself

1. Firstly **choose which email system** you would like, investigate the ones listed above and some of your own.

2. Once you have chosen an email then you can **follow these instructions**, these are for a Yahoo account, but the instructions will be very similar for all email system providers.

3. Open up the Yahoo website. www.yahoo.co.uk

4. Click on the top right Mail icon.

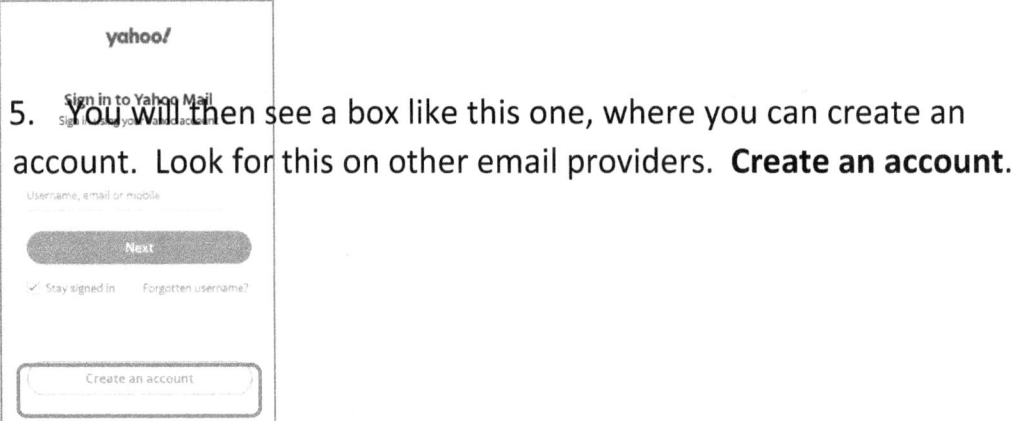

5. You will then see a box like this one, where you can create an account. Look for this on other email providers. **Create an account**.

6. You will then see the set-up page, this is where you will fill in your details that you will use for your email account. Click in each area and type in the details.

Enter you full name here; first and second name, i.e. Matt Jones.

You will be able to choose your email address name at the beginning of the email. The rest will be made up of the email provider and

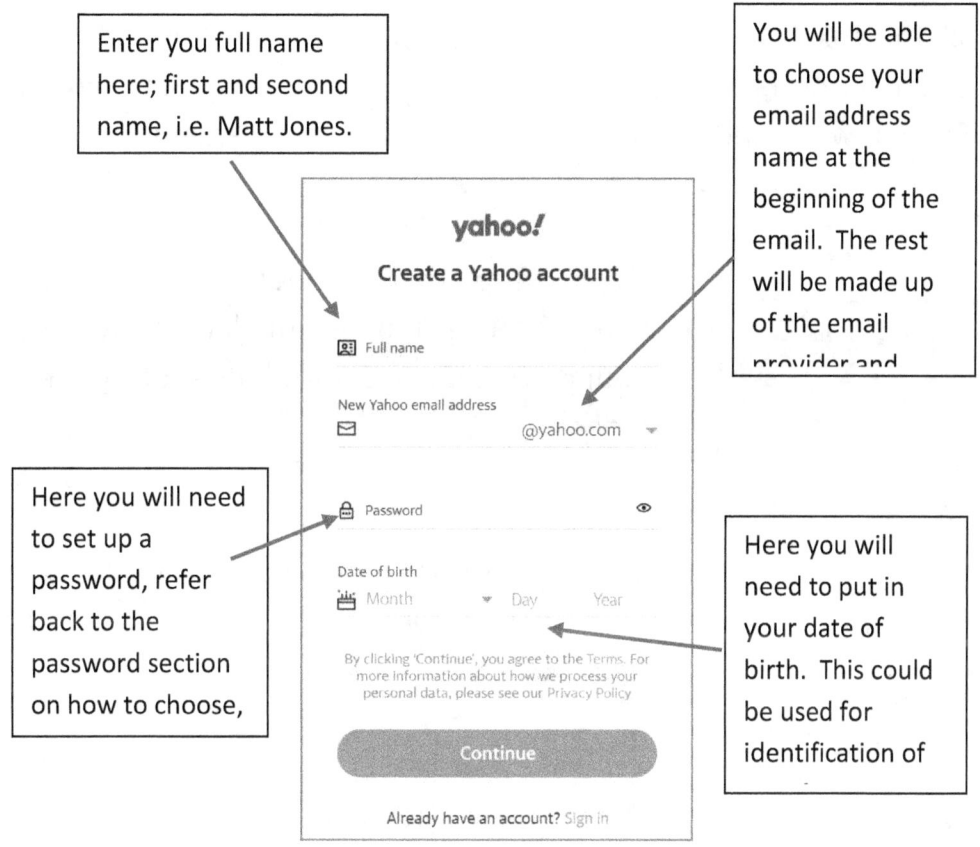

Here you will need to set up a password, refer back to the password section on how to choose,

Here you will need to put in your date of birth. This could be used for identification of

Click on continue when you have filled in your details.

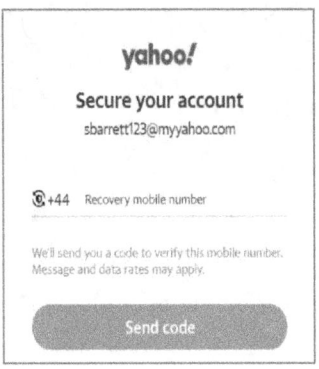

7. Here you will need to enter in your mobile phone number. This is used for authentication, to make sure it is you who is trying to access your email account.

8. Type in your mobile number and click on Send code.

9. Tick the box I'm not a  robot and click on Continue, so make sure you have your mobile with you when setting up an email account.

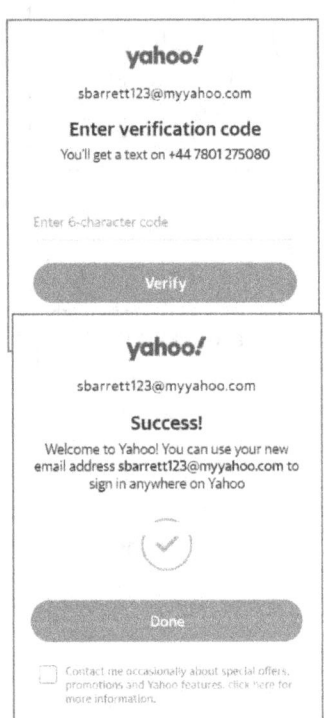

10. Type in the number that was sent to your mobile, you will have a time limit to do this, usually around 30 minutes sometimes shorter. Then click on Verify.

11. Click on Done, you can tick the contact me occasionally if you wish to receive emails about special offers or leave blank.

12. Now you need to read the email policy of Yahoo or whichever provider you have chosen and click on Accept all.

13. Then you may be asked to personalise your inbox. Run through making your choices and selections and then clicking on Next. If you do not know what choices to make just click through on Next and leave the options as they are.

See Email Layout sheet on the next page to see how the Yahoo email is laid out.

Email layout

Here you can see how many new message you have, **1**.

When the Inbox is highlighted the messages will appear here with the newest at the top of the list, in bold text.

Your name is here.

This is the **Inbox**, this is where all of your messages arrive.

When you send a message the message is put into **Sent**.

To send an email click on **Compose**, this will open up a new email.

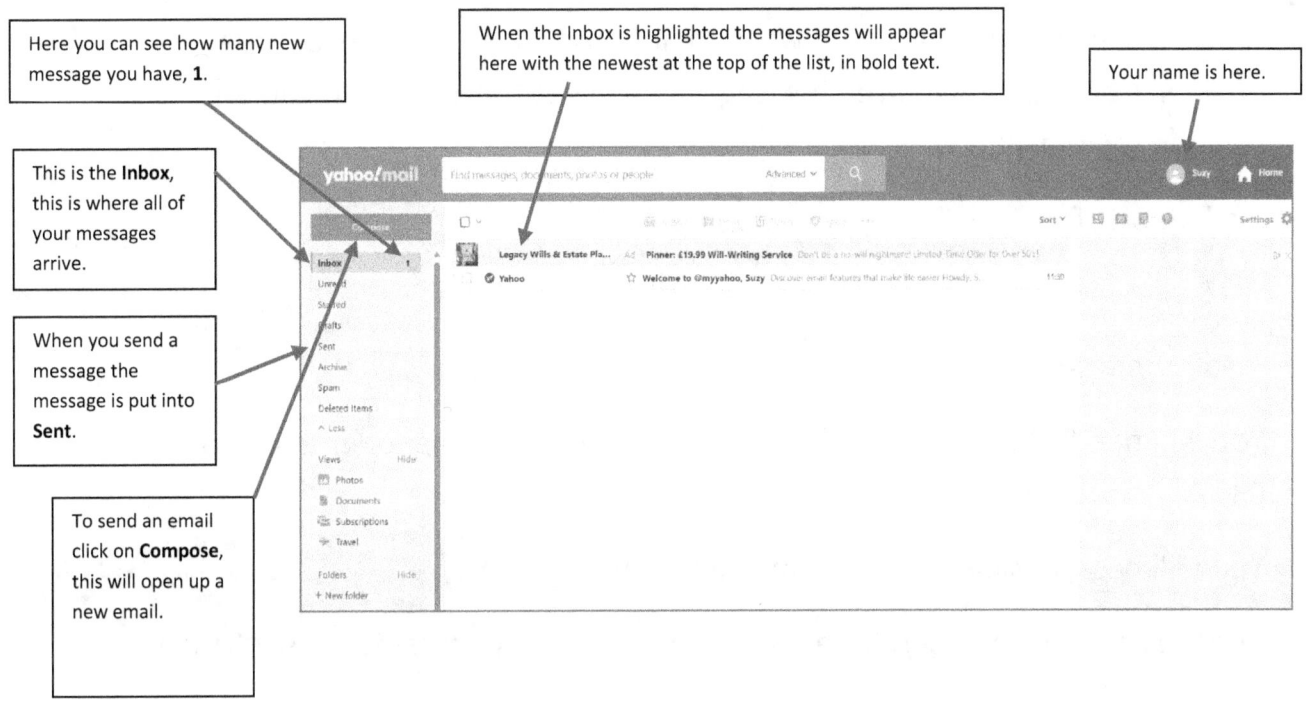

How to send an email

There are a few things you will need before you start to send an email to someone.

You will need the persons email address. This is usually lowercase but not case sensitive, this means you could write their email address as these three examples below and all three messages would get to the person you are sending the email to.

JOEBLOGGS@GMAIL.CO.UK

JoeBloggs@GMail.co.uk

joebloggs@email.co.uk

You will need to have an email provider (as the one we signed into on page 63).

You will need to sign into your email account.

Choose any web browser, here are some examples, Microsoft Edge, Mozilla, FireFox or Google Chrome.

Type in your email provider into the address bar at the top of the page and press Enter. i.e. yahoo mail

Then **Sign into** your account, using your username and password set up earlier.

Once signed in, click on Compose, or new email. Here below is the New message box.

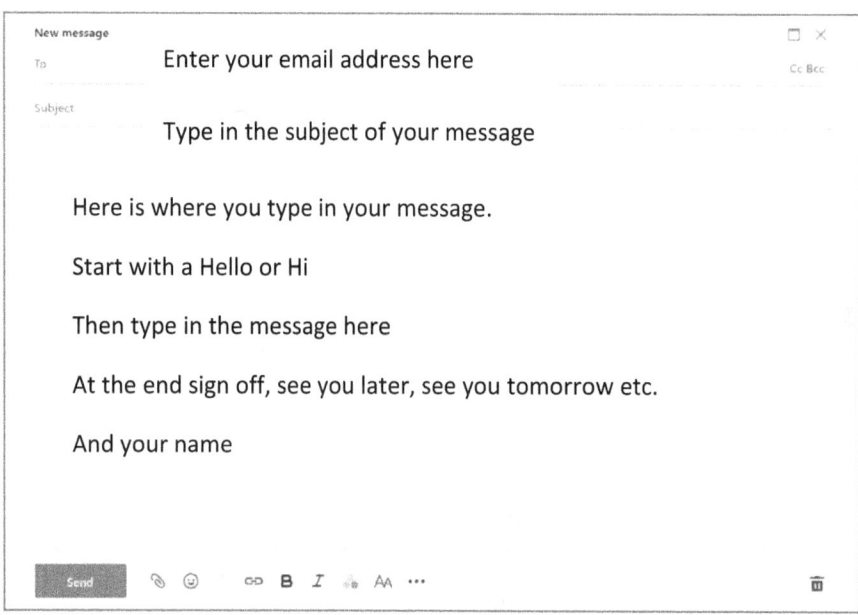

> **Football tonight**
>
> Recipients joebloggs@gmail.co.uk ×
>
> Football tonight
>
> Hi Rishi
>
> I wanted to ask you if you could give me a lift to football practice tonight. I can be ready for 7pm if that's ok?
>
> See you later.
>
> Joe

Here is an example of the email I have just created.

Top tips for writing an email

1. Write a meaningful subject link, not too long, keep it simple.
2. Keep the email focused, don't use text talk, e.g. lol, btw.
3. Avoid attachments if they are not needed.
4. Identify yourself clearly if you are writing an email for the first time.
5. Be kind, don't use CAPITAL LETTERS it is a form of shouting on email.
6. Proofread your email and use the spellcheck and grammar checks.

Review Six – Emailing:

Let's see what you have learnt so far about Emailing.

You can choose to write the answers in the book in pencil then you can re-do this review after a few month's more of practice.

1. Circle the items below which are emails.

   Ravvipatel@bbc.co.uk   paulsmith@virgin.com

   www.metro.co.uk   Goodmorning.co.uk

   HelgaG@gmail.co.uk

   www.bbc.co.uk   www.amazon.co.uk

2. If you wish to set up an email account, what do you have to do? Underline the correct answer.

   You have to sign up   **You have to sign in**

3. What do you have to include in a password? Write as many things as you can remember here.

   ----

4. Once you have logged into your email account and would like to send a new email what do you click on, circle all ones that you think are correct.

   Login

   Compose   Inbox   Sent   Subject   New email

5. Which web browser should you use to sign into your email account?

   _____

We have covered all the basics of using a computer here is a review;

- **Computer hardware**
- **Basic Input devices**
- **Computer Keyboard**
- **Digital Mouse**
- **Internet**
- **Browsers**
- **Search Engines**
- **Passwords**
- **Cookies**
- **Internet Safety**
- **Anti-Virus Software**
- **Computer Software**
- **Word**
- **Saving**
- **Emailing**

Here are some basic exercises for you to now practice what you have learnt.

Email Exercise 1:

Carry out this exercise to practice your emailing skills.

1. Open up your email account.

This will mean you need access to the internet, open up a web browser, type in your email provider (i.e. Yahoo or Hotmail etc.), sign in with your username and password. Click on Open new email.

2. Type in an email address.

You can type in any email address in here or you could send me an email, I can't always reply to all your emails, but I will definitely read them. info@coltechuk.com – Let me know if you are finding my book handy!

3. Type in a subject. For this example we are going to type in: Summer holidays

Remember this needs to be short and to the point, not the question you want to ask or a sentence.

4. In the main message start with a greeting, here are some examples you can use choose one and type it as below;
   - Dear
   - Hi
   - Hello

5. Drop down two lines (Press Enter, and Enter).

6. Type up the body of the email, remember to be precise, use proper sentences and punctuation.

Making use of the spell check and grammar check – right click for options!

You could type up something like this:

I hope this email finds you well, I wanted to ask you what you were doing for this year's summer holiday? I know last year you went to Croatia and I want to find out what you thought of it, where you stayed and the restaurants. You have such great ideas I wanted to see where you were thinking of going this year.

I am looking forward to seeing you on Saturday at the party.
See you there,

Sarah

7. Don't forget to sign off to, as above with See you there, and your name.

You can sign off in a number of ways, Kind regards, Regards, Best Wishes, Until tomorrow etc.

8. Once the email is set up and ready to go, check there are no spelling mistakes.
9. Click on Send to send the email.

Email Exercise 2:

Carry out this exercise to practice your emailing skills.

1. You have received this email from a friend and need to reply answering the questions they have asked.

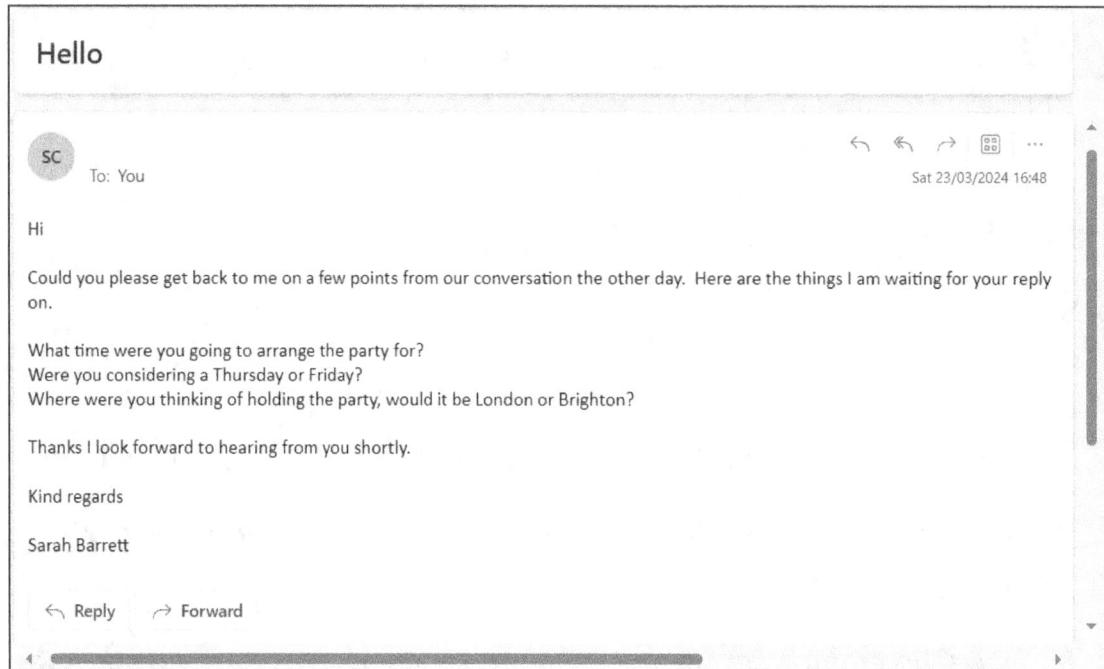

Don't forget to use your emailing skills when replying and use the same tone as the email you receive. If you receive a formal email, then reply formally. If you receive a more casual email, then reply more casually.

2. Open up a new email.
3. Use same subject as above "Hello".
4. Write up a reply to this email.

Word Exercise 1:

Carry out this exercise to practice your word skills.

1. Open up a new word document, File, Blank document.

2. Type up the following into word –

What feels like fun to me, but work to others? The mark of whether you are made for a task is not whether you love it but whether you can handle the pain of the task easier than most people.

3. Check in the Home ribbon and the font section to see what font you are typing in and the font size.

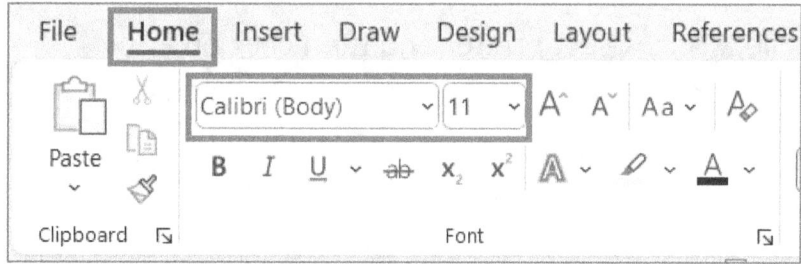

4. Type on the next line what font you are using and the point size.

5. Then change the font style to another font style by click on the down arrows next to the text, indicated by the circle on the ribbon below.

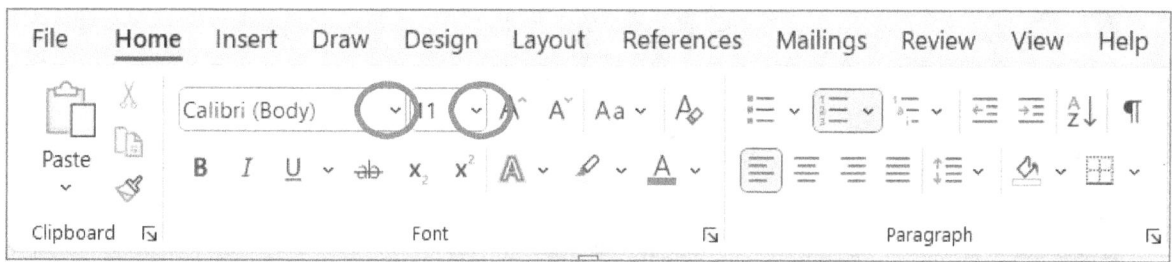

6. Type up the following text in the new font and style.

I cannot express how important it is to believe that taking one tiny—and possibly very uncomfortable—step at a time can ultimately add up to a great distance.

7. Next type up a title as below and centre it at the top of the page.

This is the first write up I have completed in word.

8. Go to the bottom of your text and insert a photo, one of your choice. Insert, Picture, Online Pictures.

9. Move down the page two lines (press enter and enter) and then type in your name.

10. Print out the page, File, Print, select printer and then click on Print.

Word exercise 2:

Carry out this exercise to practice your word skills.

1. Open up a new word document, File Blank document.

2. Type in your name, centre your name and drop down two lines.

3. Type up the following into word –

Yesterday is history, tomorrow is a mystery, but today is a gift, that is why it is called the Present. Use it enlighten yourself and enjoy your day. Just when the caterpillar thought its world was over it became a butterfly. Become a butterfly.

4. Insert a photo of a butterfly onto the page.

5. Insert, Picture, Online Pictures.

6. Type up the following two lines down from your butterfly picture. Making sure you bold the text where it is bold and italicise the text as shown below.

A **butterfly** is a flying insect of the order *'Lepidoptera'* (an order of insects with broad wings which have minute overlapping scales). In **Greek,** *'Lepidoptera'* means *'scaled wings'*. This order belongs to the superfamily *'Hesperioidea'* or *'Skippers'* as they are commonly called. **'Skippers differ from butterflies'** in that they have thicker bodies, better eyes, stronger wing muscles and hooked-back antennae.

7. Highlight all the text and change the style and point size to Calibri, 14pt.

8. Type up today's date at the bottom of the page and centre the text.

9. Print out the page, File, Print, select printer and then click on Print.

Sarah Barrett

Yesterday is history, tomorrow is a mystery, but today is a gift, that is why it is called the Present. Use it enlighten yourself and enjoy your day. Just when the caterpillar thought its world was over it became a butterfly. Become a butterfly.

A **butterfly** is a flying insect of the order *'Lepidoptera'* (an order of insects with broad wings which have minute overlapping scales). In **Greek**, *'Lepidoptera'* means *'scaled wings'*. This order belongs to the superfamily *'Hesperioidea'* or *'Skippers'* as they are commonly called. 'Skippers **differ from butterflies** in that they have thicker bodies, better eyes, stronger wing muscles and hooked-back antennae.

21st March 2024

Internet Searching Exercise 1:

Carry out these exercises to practice your internet searching skills.
Get onto the Internet, at home in the library or a friend's house.
You can use any web browser to do this, Edge, Chrome or FireFox etc.

Use Google Search, or Bing Search engine to find the site or just type in the company name into the Address Bar at the top of the webpage and press Enter. Either way will work, once on the page you will have to use the filters, searches on that webpage to find the information required and then write it into the boxes on this page or print out the page the choice is yours. If you get lost within a webpage you can usually click on the company logo to get back to the homepage and then you can start filtering again.

Task A

1. Use a search engine to find the website called "**Workaway**".
2. Go to **'host list'** and look up your favourite destination that you would like to travel to.
3. If possible, filter your search by entering the keyword that is close to your area of expertise or interests e.g. **'gardening', construction', 'cooking', and 'sport'.**
4. Print the page if you have access to a printer.

Task B

1. Use a search engine and find the website called "**Gumtree**".
2. Find the tab called **'Community'** and look up what "language and skills swap" has to offer.
3. Print an offer related to the skill you can swap or a skill that you would like to learn.

Task C

1. Use a search engine and find the website called '**Transport for London**'.
2. Find out how to plan a journey from your home to your place of work or a friend's house.
3. Print a page with the itinerary if you have access to a printer.

Internet Searching Exercise 2:

Carry out these exercises to practice your internet searching skills.
Get onto the Internet, at home in the library or a friend's house.
You can use any web browser to do this, Edge, Chrome or FireFox etc.

These are all searches and finding information on websites so you can use Google Search, Bing Search engine to find the site or just type in the company name into the Address Bar at the top of the webpage and press Enter. Either way will work, once on the page you will have to use the filters, searches on that webpage to find the information required and then write it into the boxes on this page or print out the page the choice is yours.

Task D

1. Use a search engine to navigate to **'Future Learn'** website.
2. Filter courses by category and choose an area of interest to you.
3. Choose a short course that you could do.
4. Print a relevant page if you have a printer available to use.

Task E

1. Search for the **'Open University'** and look for free courses they may offer.
2. Pick one of the categories.
3. Choose a course that is of interest to you.
4. Print a relevant page if you have a printer available to use.

Task F

1. Use Bing Search engine to find **'National Careers Service'**.
2. Navigate to Assess your skills.
3. Navigate down to Assess your skills and careers and carry out the 5-10 mins test.

Keyboard – Exercise 1:

1. Login into a PC with a username and password, use your local library if you don't have one yourself.

2. Open up a Web browser; Microsoft Edge, Google Chrome, Firefox etc.

3. Search for Typing club.

4. You are looking for this website:

www.typingclub.com

5. All you need to do is click on **Start typing.**

6. You can take a placement test if you have typed before so you can see how accurate and speed.

7. Or you can click on Lesson 1 to begin, this is a video so you will need sound for this, if you haven't got sound you can skip to lesson 2 or just watch without sound as sound is not necessary to understand where the home row positions are.

8. Keep typing 10 mins a day, and you will soon pick up speed and accuracy, don't rush to start slow and steady is best.

9. If you would like to track your progress you will need to sign up to the site and log in before you start your practice.

10. To sign up, click on the Login button on the top right, then at the bottom of the next page choose sign up. You will need an email address and you will have to set up a password.

Good luck on your typing journey!

Internet Safety Exercise 1:

This is an exercise in searching webpages and finding information.

In this exercise you will use the National Cyber Security Centre site and find out the information below.

Don't forget when navigating around a website, you can use the back button on the Address bar to go back to the previous page. Or if you wish to go to the homepage, click on the company name;

1. Use any web browser and search for this site; *National Cyber Security Centre*;
   National Cyber Security Centre - NCSC.GOV.UK

   Once on the site accept all the cookies (Accept optional cookies).

2. Search the site for "Top tips for staying secure online". Use the magnifying glass at the top right of the website, put the details in above.

3. What can help you secure passwords? Read section and answer below.

4. How are these helpful? List two points below.

5. If you share a computer what should you not do with your passwords?

6. How do three random words help you to protect yourself online?

Mousercise

You can practice all the 5 functions of the mouse by using this great website.

How to access it using the Internet

Open up a web browser, search for **'Mousercise'** and then get started on the exercises.

OR type this into the Address bar:

www.pbclibrary.org/mousing/mousercise.htm

Happy Mousercising!!

Typing

Learn how to touch type in daily 10 minute practices. It is be very handy to be able to type without looking at the keys whilst you type, this is called touch typing. There are many webpages where you can do this, this is one I found to be very handy. If you sign into the site (with a username and password), you can track your progress, best finger, speed and accuracy of your typing.

www.typingclub.com

See page 80 for keyboard exercise using this site.

Don't forget there is only one rule – Don't look down!

How to sign into Office 365 – (you can try this once you feel confident using the Internet).

Follow these instructions if you wish to sign into Office 365. You will need to sign up to Office 365. There is a monthly fee, with this you will get an account, it includes an Email account, access to Word, Excel, PowerPoint and other applications.

1. You will need to open up a web browser (Microsoft Edge, Mozilla Firefox, Google Chrome).
2. Type into the address bar **'office 365 sign in'**.

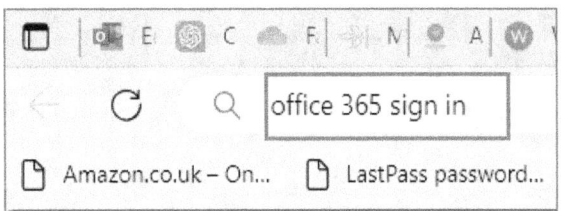

3. Click on Login Microsoft 365.
4. You will then be asked a question, if you have signed in before you will need to choose the account, or just click on Sign in.

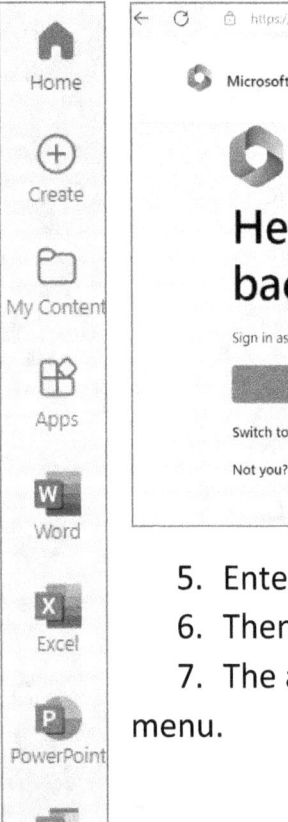

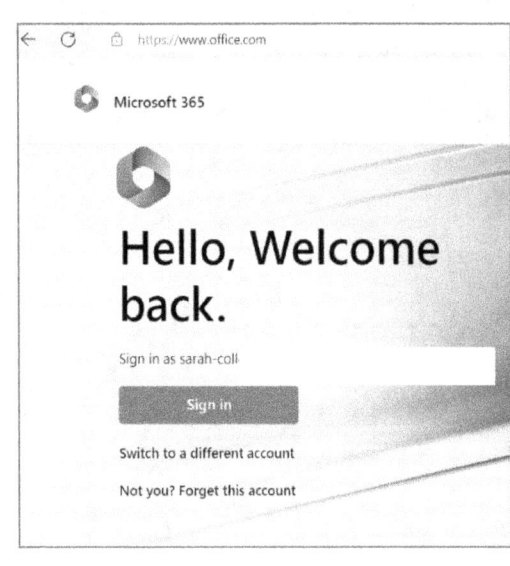

5. Enter your password.
6. Then you will get into your Office 365 account.
7. The apps you can use will be shown down the left-hand side menu.

Answers to the Reviews

Review One – Basic functions

1. Which one is a photo of a PC?

2. There are 5 functions of a mouse.
3. Yes you can buy a wireless mouse.
4. The combination of characters do you need for a password is Symbols, Capital letters, Lowercase letters and numbers only.
5. The items listed here are hardware; Webcam, ipad, Keyboard.

Review Two - Internet

1. You could have written any one of these web browsers to gain access to the Internet. Microsoft Edge, Google Chrome, Mozilla FireFox or FireFox, Safari, Opera.
2. Items you need to keep yourself save when shopping or banking online are; Secure password, Email address, Up-to-date Anti-virus software, username, unique password, padlock, padlock.
3. What is a homepage? The main page of a website where all the details of the company are found.
4. The internet is available throughout the whole world. So the answer is False it is not only available in the UK.
5. Beginning is www, company is the name of the company Amazon, and the ending is; .co.uk

---

Internet Safety Exercise 1

3. Password manager can help you secure passwords when working online.
4. Use any two of these helpful points.

a. Synchronise your passwords across your different devices, making it easier to log on whenever you are, and whatever you're using.
   b. Help spot fake websites, which will protect you from phishing attacks.
   c. Let you know if you're re-using the same password across different accounts.
   d. Notify you if your passwords appear within a known data breach so you know if you need to change it.
   e. Work across platforms, so you could (for example) use a single password manager that would work for your iPhone and your Windows desktop.
5. You should never save your passwords into your browser if you share a computer with either family or housemates.
6. If you choose three random words you can use these to create a unique password that is hard to crack.

Review Three – Password

1. 12 characters long, lowercase letters, uppercase letters, numbers and symbols.
2. Date of birth of yourself or any of your family members, names of your family, names of pets, favourite colours, favourite bands etc.
3. Logging into your bank account, logging into your Outlook mail account.
4. Your password must always be long with no mention of your personal details.
5. Use a password manager or a password formula.
6. Password manager, password formula, a password that is easy to remember but hard to crack.

Review Four – Word and Software

1. Where can you find MS Word software? These are the answers.
   Under the Windows key
   Pinned to the taskbar

Shortcut on the desktop
2. Word does have a spellcheck.
3. The software packages that were listed were; Word Excel, PowerPoint, Outlook.
4. These are Font styles, the way the style of the writing looks.
5. This is the symbol to centre text.

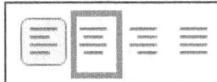

6. This is the symbol is to italics text.

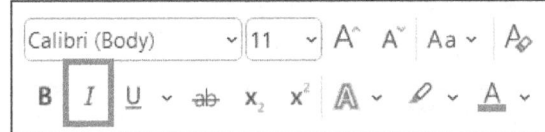

7. This is the symbol to change the font colour.

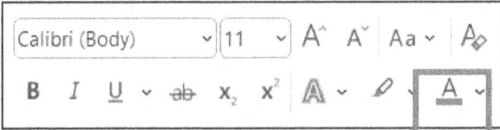

8. The insert tab is the one you select to insert photos into a word document.

Review Five – Saving

1. Word, Excel, PowerPoint and Outlook
2. USB Stick, Cloud storage, Computer Desktop, Computer C Drive
3. Box Storage, Drop box, Google Drive
4. Take it away and use it in another computer, Backing up files

Review Six – Emailing

1. Ravvipatel@bbc.co.uk   paulsmith@virgin.com   HelgaG@gmail.co.uk
2. You have to sign up.
3. 12 characters, lowercase, uppercase, symbols, numbers
4. New Email, Compose.
5. You can use any web browser.

Handy keyboard layout

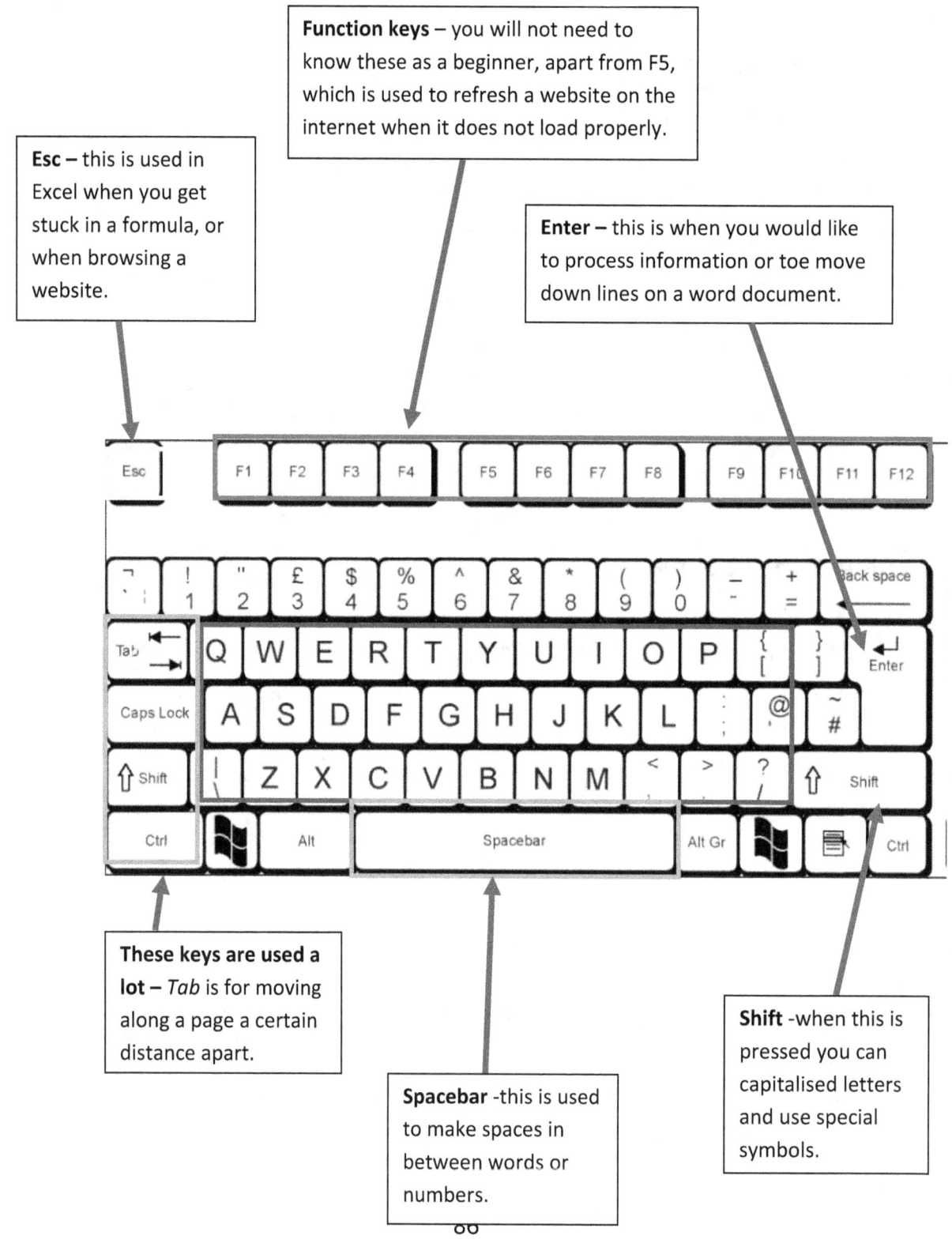

Function keys – you will not need to know these as a beginner, apart from F5, which is used to refresh a website on the internet when it does not load properly.

Esc – this is used in Excel when you get stuck in a formula, or when browsing a website.

Enter – this is when you would like to process information or toe move down lines on a word document.

These keys are used a lot – *Tab* is for moving along a page a certain distance apart.

Spacebar -this is used to make spaces in between words or numbers.

Shift -when this is pressed you can capitalised letters and use special symbols.

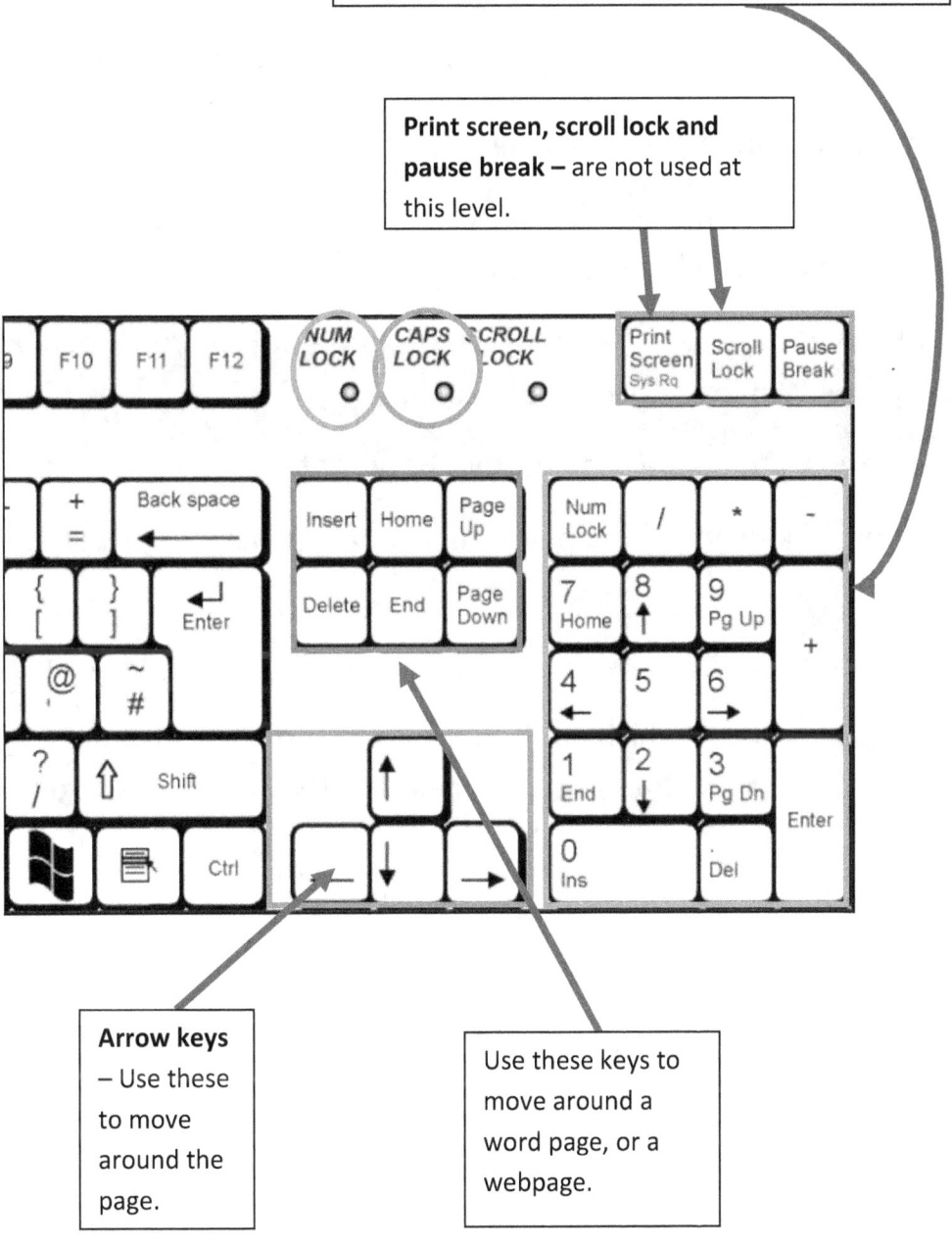

Web browsers Quick Tip Sheet

To get onto the Internet you use what is called a browser. There are many types you can use some of which you may have heard of. Search for the browsers and draw in the matching logos.

    Firefox   Microsoft Edge   Safari   Google Chrome   Opera

Some information about each browser

Firefox use to be called Mozilla Firefox but is now known as just Firefox. It was voted best all-round web browser in 2023.

Microsoft Edge this use to be called Microsoft Internet Explorer, voted best web browser for Windows 10 and 11 in 2023.

Safari this is known to be the best internet browser for Apple computer users.

Google Chrome is known to be the best functional browser, arguably the most common.

Opera is the most diverse browser, can be used on PC's and Apple computers.

You may have a choice to which one you use to get onto the Internet, you may not. Some companies or libraries have a main one they always use, you will have to use this.

Notes:…..

Introduction to Shortcut Keys

This is an introduction to shortcut keys. These are very handy to use when you get started using the computer. You will need to highlight the text you would like to use first then use the shortcut key to perform the action. I have left space at the end so you can add in your own handy shortcut keys.

Control + C	Use this to copy items in Word, Excel, PowerPoint etc.	Control + V	Use this to Paste your copied items.
Control + X	Use this to Cut the text or item out of the document or presentation etc.	Control + S	Use this to Save a document.
Control + Z	This is used to Undo a task.	Control + P	Use this to print pages.

Glossary

Address line – this is the area on a webpage where you can type in the web address of a company you wish to visit.

Android phone – this is a phone that is made by any number of suppliers such as Samsung, Huawei, Google etc.

Anti-virus software – is a software program you buy that secures your computer from viruses and hackers.

Apple computers/ Mac – they are now known as Apple or MAC, they began in 1976 and was founded by Steve Jobs and Steve Woznaik in California.   They are a particular type of computer and they produce iPhones, Apple computers, tablets along with many other items.

Apps – this is short for application (software application). This is a **downloadable** program for a mobile device.

Backed-up – this is to do with computer files you have stored on your computer. You will need to back them up to another device in case the computer crashes and breaks down your files will be gone if you cannot access them or have them stored somewhere else – not backed-up.

Browser – a web browser is a software program that allows a user to locate, access and display web pages. In common usage, a web browser is usually shortened to browser. A Browser is used to access websites on the internet.

Characters – these are keys on the keyboard for example; a,b,c,d, 4,5,6, ?,> and they can be any type of letter, number or symbols etc.

Cookie ID Code – (it is known as a HTTP cookie or web cookie or browser cookie). It is a small piece of data (ID code) that the server sends to the users' browser when you start to use their website, it tracks where you visit and what you buy.

CPU (central processing unit) – this executes instructions from a computer program.

Devices – this can be an iPhone, a mobile phone, a tablet, a PC etc. Anything that can connect to the Internet with.

Downloadable – it is something that is downloaded from the Internet to your computer, or phone. Usually a software application.

Facebook – this is a social media site for connecting with friends, staying connected and sharing your photos and adventures with your friends. You can also join groups of like-minded people share ideas online.

F5 – refresh key on the keyboard – very useful when you need to refresh a webpage.

Hacker(s) – this is a person who breaks into a computer system. There are several reasons a person does this. It maybe to install the malware, stealing data or asking for money in a **Ransom attack**, Destroying data, disrupting a service and more. Hacking can also be done for ethical reasons such as trying to show vulnerabilities in software so it can be fixed.

Hardware – or computer hardware includes the actual parts of the computer, these include; monitor, mouse, keyboard, CPU (central processing unit), speakers etc. Think of them as things you can physically touch.

Hotspot – this is physical location where people can access the Internet, usually through wifi. Basically wifi hotspots are physical places where users can wirelessly connect their mobile devices, and tablets to the internet.

Hyperlink – sometimes known as a **Link**. This is a bit of text in a sentence that is linked to another page on a website, part of the current page or to a document. When you click on the link the website, part of the page or document opens.

Input device – this is piece of equipment used to provide data and control information, for example an input device can be a keyboard, mouse, scanner, camera etc.

iPhone – this is a phone that has been made by Apple and is a very popular mobile phone.

Link – sometimes known as a **hyperlink.** This is a word of text in a sentence that is linked to another page on a website, part of the current page or to a document. When you click on the link the website, part of the page or document it opens up.

Like – you like posts and comments on lots of popular social media sites by clicking on the "Thumbs up".

Logo – this is a symbol or small design used by a company or organisation to identify itself, its products, or services etc.

Malware – is short for malicious software, it is usually designed by hackers to steal, damage or destroy computers, computer systems or confidential information.

Mouse – this is an input device, which helps us point at any item on the screen and to draw with. You can get digital mice, ergonomic mice, wireless mice depending on your needs.

Multifactor authentication – this is used when signing into an account. You would enter in your username and password and then to check that it is you, you get a code sent to your phone and you can to type the code into the website to confirm your login details and gain access to the website.

Office 365 – this is subscription service that you pay for every month. It can also be known as Microsoft 365. You will be able to use software applications (apps) such as Word, Excel, PowerPoint and an email account using Outlook. You can sign into this account on any computer, mobile device or tablet online. To sign up use this link to get started, you will need to set up a password and you will need an email to do this. Compare All Microsoft 365 Plans (Formerly Office 365) – Microsoft Store or search for Office 365.

Online Reviews – people fill out online reviews when they have purchased something online, or visited a restaurant so people can see what the restaurant is like.

Padlock – this is shown on websites to make sure the site is secure and would be shown when signing into a website like banking, shopping where you have your card details entered.

Password – a set of characters that are used together to enable you along with your username to sign into a PC. They are usually 12 or more characters long.

PC – personal computer, the computer itself.

PC computers – these are computers that are made by any firm and will have Windows operating system on them, and usually Office Suite which contains, Word, Excel, PowerPoint and Outlook email.

Phishing – it is sending an email pretending to be from a reputable firm, such as a bank asking you to clarify information. The name comes from 'fishing' for information.

Pointer – this is shown on the computer screen which you can move around to select items and highlight text etc.

Portrait or Landscape – these are the two options *Portrait* is this format:

Landscape is this format.

Printer Drivers – are software that enables you to communicate between your computer and your printer. You can find print drivers on the internet.

Privacy settings – these are settings usually found on a social media networking website. The privacy settings allow you to control who can see your information and who cannot.

QR Code – this is a set of shapes that when you open your smartphone camera up and hoover over it, it will open a website.

Shortcut – this can be a shortcut of a program on the desktop of a computer that is easy to open instead of finding the software package and opening it.

Sign in – most PC's require access a username and password to access a computer, at work, public places for example libraries, educational places, schools and colleges, and sometimes if you share a computer at home.

Smartphones – this is not just a phone for phone calls or sending text messages, but a mobile phone that has the ability to perform many functions of a computer, they usually have **touchscreens**, internet access and run multiple **apps**.

Startup/ Boot Up – this is what it is called when the computer starts up and loads up all the computer software and programs it needs to start working. You should wait until these finish before you start to use it.

Subscribe – in a number of social media programs when people post items other people can like or subscribe the posts. Then when the person posts more items if you have subscribed you get a notification to say there is a new post.

Surf the net – this refers to using the internet and visiting different websites. Browsing around the internet and opening and using websites.

Symbols or special characters – these are included in writing passwords – an example of these are as follows: "$&(?>}{ etc.

Tabs - these are different webpages open on a browser at one time.

Touchscreens – this is a display device that allows you to interact with the computer, tablet or smartphone by touching areas on the screen with your finger. It is a useful alternative to a mouse or keyboard for moving around and using the computer.

Two step authentication – this is usually used when you are using the internet or trying to access a secure site or application. It means that you put in your username and password and to clarify as a second step the company would send you a code to a phone, or another email address which you would then put into the site to gain access. This proves that it is you trying to get into the site, as you need to have your email and phone to do this.

Username – this is usually given to you by the firm you are working for. Or if you would like to sign into a computer in the library then they would give you a username. It is a unique set of letters and characters unique to you.

User – a user is a person who uses a computer and what you are called when asking an IT professional for help.

Virus (computer) – this is a type of **malware** that when launched it starts to double in size and starts inserting its own code into software programs. If it succeeds in infecting the program it is said to be infected with a computer virus.

Web Address – this is the web address of the company you would like to visit. Each company or service has their own unique web address which is usually fully searchable.

Webpage – is a page on the World Wide Web. The pages are displayed through a web browser.

Website – consists of many webpages linked together under one name.

Wi-Fi – the best way to understand Wi-Fi is it allows computers, **smartphones**, and other devices to connect to one another, through receiving and transmitting a wireless signal.

World Wide Web – WWW, this hosts websites.

Word 365 -this is the online Word app you can use anywhere once you have signed up to Office 365, details above.

YouTube – this is a video site where you can see videos like and subscribe to the channels on almost any topic.

Thank you's

I would like to thank you for taking the time to use and read my book. I really hope you have found it helpful and will continue to use it in your future journey into using computers.

I would like to thank my husband and three daughters for all the hours that I have used to write this book and for my husband's support with the editing process.

www.ingramcontent.com/pod-product-compliance
Lightning Source LLC
Chambersburg PA
CBHW062224220526

45471CB00009B/3332